MARRIAGE:
THE ROCK ON WHICH THE FAMILY IS BUILT

WILLIAM E. MAY

MARRIAGE:

THE ROCK ON WHICH
THE FAMILY IS BUILT

IGNATIUS PRESS   SAN FRANCISCO

Cover design by Riz Boncan Marsella

© 1995 Ignatius Press
ISBN 0-89870-537-1
Library of Congress catalogue number 94-79300
Printed in the United States of America

To Pope John Paul II
The Champion of Marriage and the Family

CONTENTS

7

FOREWORD

One of the less fortunate aspects of the Year of the Family was the way the word "marriage" was studiously avoided when referring to the family. I encountered this at major occasions beyond the sphere of the Church's celebration of the Year. By exploring the riches of marriage in the Catholic tradition, Professor William E. May provides a powerful reply to attempts to minimalize marriage. His title expresses the natural relationship established by the Creator: *Marriage: The Rock on Which the Family Is Built.*

Having worked with Professor May through the Pontifical Council for the Family, I have come to appreciate and value his considered judgments. His thorough scholarship and breadth of vision is evident in this book. At the same time, he brings to his work not only the skills of a notable moralist, but also his own experience as a Catholic husband, father and grandfather.

Professor May draws on the magisterial sources of the modern popes, and he includes a timely and forthright defense of Pope Paul VI and *Humanae vitae*. In particular, he shares with his readers a profound and wide knowledge of the teaching and thought of the Holy Father Pope John Paul II. I commend his useful overview of the Holy Father's *Letter to Families*. This great gift of the Pope to families is encouraging married couples to rediscover the "rock" of the sacramental bond and communion of life and love that Christ the Bridegroom imparts.

Professor May enjoys great prestige, merited by so many studies containing profound and faithful teaching and through his tireless service in the meetings to which he is invited in different nations. It is thus most encouraging to see a professor of such authority present a book which is solid, modern, and faithful, responding to what the Holy Father says in *Familiaris Consortio*, 31: "In fulfillment of their specific role, theologians are called upon to provide enlightenment and a deeper understanding, and their contribution is of incomparable value and represents a unique and highly meritorious service to the family and humanity."

Alfonso Cardinal López Trujillo

President of the Pontifical Council for the Family

INTRODUCTION

I believe that marriage, as the subtitle of this book proclaims, is the rock on which the family is built. It is so, as I hope to show, precisely because marriage is a person-affirming, love-enabling, life-giving, and sanctifying reality. It is an integral component of God's wise and loving plan for human existence and has been raised by his Son Jesus Christ to the dignity of a sacrament of the new law of grace and love.

I believe that Pope John Paul II, to whom this book is dedicated, will go down in history as the champion of marriage and the family. From his earliest days as a priest, he has thought deeply about the beauty of marriage and the human significance of family life. This is reflected in the plays that he wrote as a young man, in particular *The Jeweler's Shop*, in the masterful study on *Love and Responsibility* that he wrote during the years he was a professor of ethics, and above all in the many discourses and writings on marriage and family that have been the hallmark of his pontificate. These began with his famous Wednesday audiences on the "theology of the body". These audiences, which began on September 9, 1979, and continued until November 28, 1984, have been published in four volumes: *Original Unity of Man and Woman: Catechesis on the Book of Genesis*, *"Blessed Are the Pure of Heart": Catechesis on the Sermon on the Mount, Reflections on "Humanae Vitae"*, and *The Theology of Marriage and Celibacy: Catechesis on Marriage and Celibacy in the Light of the Resurrection of the Body*. In 1981, in responding to the 1980 Synod of Bishops, he published his marvelous Apostolic Exhortation on the Role of the Family in the World Today (*Familiaris consortio*), a beautiful work offering a veritable *"summa"* of Catholic teaching on marriage and the family. In February 1994, to mark the International Year of the Family, he issued his wonderful *Letter to Families,* a work expressing in a loving and even passionate way his superb appreciation of the beauty of marriage and family in the plan of God for man's salvation. When this letter was first made available in English, I got copies for all my children. After I read it, I immediately wrote to them and urged them to read this beautiful letter. For the two who are already married, it offers a tremendous challenge for them—and for all married persons—to treasure the vocation God has given them and to be faithful to it. For the five who are not married, it offers one of the finest things available to help them prepare either for marriage or for living chastely as single persons who find their "home" in their family. Truly John Paul II is the pope of marriage and the family.

In addition, Pope John Paul II, energetically responding to the desires of the 1985 extraordinary Synod of Bishops, saw to the preparation and promulgation of a new *Catechism of the Catholic Church* in order to give to the people of God a marvelous source for what he himself describes as "a catechesis renewed at the living sources of the faith" (Apostolic Constitution *Fidei Despositum,* on the publication of the *Catechism of the Catholic Church* prepared following the Second Vatican Ecumenical Council). This *Catechism* provides, in a brief, beautifully written chapter (nos. 1601–66), an accurate and challenging summary of the Church's understanding of marriage. In addition, it beautifully describes the virtue of chastity and the authentic character of the love of husband and wife (nos. 2331–400).

In this book I hope that I have been able to summarize the major truths proclaimed by the Church, in particular by Pope John Paul II, on marriage and the family. I believe that the Church's teaching on marriage and family can be summed up as follows. Marriage is the rock on which the human family, indispensable for "civilization of love", is built. The reason why marriage is this rock is that it is, according to God's wise and loving plan for human existence, a person-affirming, love-enabling, life-giving, and sanctifying reality. What I have written here is intended to show the truth of all this.

The first Chapter, "Marriage: A Person-affirming, Love-enabling, Life-giving, and Sanctifying Reality", attempts to provide an overview of the reasons why marriage is indeed the rock on which the family is built. In it I seek to provide a synthesis of the understanding of marriage in the Catholic tradition so beautifully developed by Pope John Paul II and presented in the *Catechism of the Catholic Church*. In doing so, I also endeavor to formulate moral criteria for the family today. The following chapters seek to deepen this understanding of marriage.

The second chapter, "Marriage and the Complementarity of Male and Female", explores the complementarity of the sexes, showing how this complementarity is revealed in and is essential to the one-flesh union of man and woman in marriage. Its purpose is to show that the complementarity of male and female contributes to the meaning of marriage as person-affirming, love-enabling, life-giving, and sanctifying.

Chapter Three, devoted to an analysis of Pope Paul VI's Encyclical *Humanae vitae,* is concerned primarily with the meaning of marriage as a love-enabling and life-giving reality. It is also intended to show the rich personalism at the heart of this Encyclical, a personalism which, as I hope to show, has been appreciated, developed, and deepened by the thought of Pope John Paul II. This true personalism is, as will be seen, utterly at odds with the pseudo-personalism—in reality, a dualism that disparages the human body and bodily life and is reminiscent of the ancient heresies of gnosticism and Manichaeanism—advanced by those who champion contraception as a morally legitimate means for deepening conjugal love and exercising responsible parenthood.

Chapter Four is an in-depth analysis of the issues raised by the ability of contemporary man to generate new human life in the laboratory. Its purpose is to show that the only way properly to respect the dignity of human life is to receive it as a "gift", crowning the one-flesh union of husband and wife in the intimacy of the marital act—to "beget" it in an act of spousal love. It is an endeavor to explore more deeply the meaning of marriage as a *life-giving* reality, one that welcomes new human life as a person equal in dignity to its progenitors and that does not dishonor it by considering it as a product inferior to its producers and subject to quality controls.

The fifth chapter is concerned with Christian marriage as a

sanctifying reality, as a domestic Church. It is, in essence, a commentary on a major section of Pope John Paul II's Apostolic Exhortation *Familiaris consortio.*

In an appendix, I offer an overview of Pope John Paul II's beautiful *Letter to Families.* I have sought to synthesize the teaching in this magnificent, passionate document by considering, first, the Holy Father's understanding of the "civilization of love" and, second, by organizing the major ideas set forth in the document, which clearly affirms that marriage is the rock on which the family is built, around the themes of marriage as a person-affirming, love-enabling, life-giving, and sanctifying reality.

An earlier draft of Chapter One was delivered as a lecture, entitled "Moral Criteria for the Family of Today", at the I Congreso Panamericano sobre Familia y Educacion in Monterrey, Mexico, May 23–26, 1994. An earlier version of Chapter Three was presented at the Symposium "Love and Life: The Twenty-Fifth Anniversary of *Humanae Vitae*" in Omaha, Nebraska, July 25–30, 1993. Chapter Two appeared originally in *Anthropotes: Rivista sulla persona e la famiglia* in 1992, a journal published by the Istituto Giovanni Paolo II per studi su Matrimonio e Famiglia in Rome. Chapter Four, which develops ideas which I had set forth in some previous studies, is included in *Catholic Studies in Bioethics,* edited by Kevin W. Wildes, S.J. (Dordrecht, Holland: Kluver Academic Publishers, 1995). Chapter Five, which was written in such close cooperation with my wife, Patricia, that she should be regarded as its coauthor, was originally given at the 1993 Annual Convention of the Fellowship of Catholic Scholars and was published in the Proceedings of that Convention in 1994. I am grateful for permission to use this material here. The Appendix, offering an overview of Pope John Paul II's *Letter to Families,* is published here for the first time.

On March 25, 1995 Pope John Paul II issued a new Encyclical, *Evangelium vitae.* Its final chapter, "For a New Culture of Human Life", highlights the truth that the family, rooted in marriage, is indeed the "sanctuary of life". I hope that this book will illumine this truth.

1

Marriage: A Person-affirming, Love-enabling, Life-giving, and Sanctifying Reality

Introduction

Families, and particularly children, are gravely at risk today. This was frankly acknowledged in the Report, entitled *Beyond Rhetoric: A New American Agenda for Children and Families,* issued in the summer of 1991 by a National Commission on Children established in 1987 by the Congress and President of the United States. The Commission's Report is grim. The following heartrending findings of the Commission will help us appreciate the magnitude of the difficulties confronting us:

1. Today, one in four children in the United States is raised by just one parent, usually a divorced or unmarried mother. Many grow up without the consistent presence of a father in their lives. . . .

2. Illicit drugs and the wanton violence they spawn have ravaged U.S. communities, large and small . . . with devastating consequences for children of all ages. . . . Many are abandoned at birth by parents who are too impaired to want them or care for them. . . .

3. [A] child need not be economically poor to be impoverished in America today. A poverty of spirit touches every child, at whatever income level, who does not receive the time, attention,

and guidance he or she needs and wants from parents and other caring adults.[1]

The Commission likewise noted the social problems caused by the alarming decline in the proportion of children to the general population. This decline is attributable to a dramatic fall in the birthrate, caused by the widespread practice in the United States of contraception[2] and, a matter on which the Commission's Report is silent, of abortion. For the past decade, in fact, more than a million and a half unborn children have been aborted each year in the United States; and in some American cities, including the nation's capital, more babies are aborted annually than are born.

These sobering statistics give us a glimpse of the difficulties facing families in the United States today. Although the portrait drawn may not be replicated precisely in other countries, there is no doubt that contraception, abortion, and divorce, with their impact on children and families, characterize the affluent nations of the West and are being vigorously promoted elsewhere. There is an urgent need for what Pope John Paul II calls "the civilization of love"[3] to take root in the hearts of contemporary men and women and for families *to be what they are: communities of loving service to life and society.*

Here I will show that marriage, the rock upon which the family is built, is a *person-affirming, love-enabling, life-giving, and sanctifying reality.* In doing so I will develop some moral criteria for the family today.

[1] *Beyond Rhetoric: A New American Agenda for Children and Families* (Final Report of the National Commission on Children) (Washington, DC: National Commission on Children, 1991), pp. 4–5. On this also see David Blankenhorn, *Fatherless America* (New York: Basic Books, 1995).

[2] *Beyond Rhetoric,* p. 16.

[3] See his *Letter to Families,* February 2, 1994, pt 1, nos. 6–17.

Marriage: The Rock on Which the Family Is Built

The first and most basic moral criterion (1) for the family of today—and of *every* day and age—is this: *The family must be rooted in the marriage of one man and one woman.* This is clearly affirmed in the *Catechism of the Catholic Church,* which states that "a man and a woman united in marriage, together with their children, form a family. This institution is prior to any recognition by public authority, which has an obligation to recognize it. It should be considered the *normal reference point* by which the different forms of family relationship are to be evaluated" (*Catechism of the Catholic Church,* no. 2202; emphasis added; cf. Pope John Paul II, *Letter to Families,* no. 17). Although the reasons for this should be obvious, this basic truth, unfortunately, seems difficult for many of our contemporaries to understand. Thus I will now try to show why this is such a basic normative truth by reflecting on the relationship between marriage and the generation of human life and by articulating other basic moral criteria for the family of today.

Marriage and the Generation of Human Life

If the human race is to continue, new human beings—new persons—must come into existence. Although it is possible today to "make" human babies in the laboratory,[4] we all know that human babies come into existence through the genital union of a man and a woman and that this is surely the usual way that new human beings come to be.

A human being, no matter how he comes to be, is something precious and good, a person, a being of incalculable value, worthy of respect, a bearer of inviolable rights, a being who *ought to be loved.*[5] But it is *not* good for new human life to come into

---

[4] This subject will be explored in depth below, in Chapter Four.

[5] This truth, of course, is a matter of Catholic faith, which holds that human beings, alone of all material things, have been made in the image and likeness of

existence through the random copulation of nonmarried males and females. This is not good, precisely because nonmarried males and females have failed to *capacitate* themselves, through their own free choices, to receive this life lovingly, to nourish it humanely, and to educate it in the love and service of God and man.[6]

Practically all civilized societies, until very recently, rightly regarded it irresponsible for unattached men and women to generate human life through their acts of fornication, and it is a sign of a new barbarism, completely opposed to the "civilization of love", that many today now assert the "right" of "live-in lovers" and of single men and women to have children, whether the fruit of their coupling or the "product" of new "reproductive" technologies.[7]

Nonmarried individuals do not have the *right* to generate human life precisely because they are not married. They refuse to give themselves unconditionally to one another and to respect the

---

God and are called to life eternal with him. But this is also a truth that can be known and defended philosophically. I cannot, of course, do so here, but I call attention to a remarkable work by the philosopher Mortimer Adler, *The Difference of Man and the Difference It Makes* (New York and Cleveland: Meridian, 1968). Adler rightly argues that "the dignity of man is the dignity of the human being as a person—a dignity not possessed by things.... The dignity of man as a person underlies the moral imperative that enjoins us never to use other human beings merely as a means, but always to respect them as ends to be served" (p. 17).

See also Karol Wojtyla (Pope John Paul II), *Love and Responsibility*, trans. H. T. Willetts (New York: Farrar, Straus, and Giroux, 1981; reprinted, San Francisco: Ignatius Press, 1993), p. 41. "The person is the kind of good which does not admit of use and cannot be treated as an object of use and as such the means to an end.... The person is a good towards which the only proper and adequate attitude is love."

[6] Centuries ago St. Augustine rightly observed that one of the chief *goods* of marriage is children, who are "to be received lovingly, nourished humanely, and educated religiously", i.e., in the love and service of God and man. See his *De genesi ad literam*, 9, 7 (PL 34, 397).

[7] I recognize that unmarried individuals can at times care properly for their children, and parents who become single because of widowhood or abandonment or other causes seek heroically in many instances to provide for their children, and they both need and deserve the support of the larger human community and the Church to exercise their responsibilities. But this is not the way things *ought to be,* and nothing can substitute for the home that loving spouses are able to give their children.

"goods" or "blessings" of marriage, among which are children and faithful conjugal love. But married men and women, precisely because they have given themselves to one another in marriage, have made themselves *fit* to generate human life.[8] By freely choosing to give themselves unreservedly to one another they have given themselves the identity of husbands and wives who *can*, together, welcome a child lovingly and give it the home it needs if it is to take root and grow. Because they have committed themselves to one another and to the "goods" or "blessings" of marriage, they have capacitated themselves to nourish the child to whom they can give life humanely and to educate it in the love and service of God and man.

Here an analogy may be helpful. I do not have the right to diagnose sick people and prescribe medicines for them. I do not have this right because I have not freely chosen to study medicine and discipline myself so that I can acquire the knowledge and skills needed to do these tasks. But doctors, who have freely chosen to submit themselves to the discipline of studying medicine and of developing the skills necessary to practice it, do have this right. They have freely chosen to make themselves *fit* to do what doctors are supposed to do. Similarly, married men and women have, by freely choosing to marry, made themselves *fit* to do what husbands and wives are supposed to do; and among the things that husbands and wives are supposed to do is to give life to new human beings and to provide them with the home they need. Thus a second (2) moral criterion for the family today is this: *Children, who are persons equal in dignity to their mothers and fathers, are to be begotten in the loving embrace of husband and wife,* and not through acts of fornication and adultery, nor are they to be "made" in the laboratory and treated as products inferior to their producers.

---

[8] On this, see *Humanae vitae,* no. 12.

Marriage: A Person-affirming, Love-enabling, Life-giving, and Sanctifying Reality

I. Marriage: A Person-affirming Reality

Marriage comes into existence when a man and a woman, for-swearing all others, through an "act of irrevocable personal consent"[9] freely give themselves to one another. At the heart of the act establishing marriage is a free, self-determining choice on the part of the man and the woman, through which they give themselves a new and lasting identity. This man becomes this woman's *husband,* and she becomes his *wife,* and together they become *spouses.* Prior to this act of irrevocable personal consent, the man and the woman are separate individuals, replaceable and substitutable in each other's lives. But, in and through this act, they make each other unique and irreplaceable.[10] The man and the woman are not, for each other, *replaceable and substitutable individuals* but are rather *irreplaceable and non-substitutable persons* (with the emphasis on "persons"). Thus marriage, far from being a legalistic or extrinsic limitation on the freedom of men and women or an empty formality, is indeed, as Pope John Paul II reminds us, "an interior requirement of the covenant of conjugal love which is publicly affirmed as unique and exclusive".[11]

The *Catechism of the Catholic Church,* reflecting on this cru-cially important matter, declares that the consent to marriage

> consists in a "human act by which the partners mutually give themselves to each other": "I take you to be my wife"—"I take

---

[9] On this, see Vatican Council II, *Gaudium et spes* [Pastoral Constitution on the Church in the Modern World], no. 48.

[10] Here the words of the late German Protestant theologian Helmut Thielicke are pertinent. He wrote: "Not uniqueness establishes the marriage, but the marriage establishes the uniqueness." *The Ethics of Sex* (New York: Harper & Row, 1963), p. 108.

[11] Pope John Paul II, Apostolic Exhortation *Familiaris consortio,* no. 11. John Paul II completes this sentence by writing: "in order to live in complete fidelity to the plan of God".

you to be my husband" [*Gaudium et spes,* no. 48; cf. *Code of Canon Law,* can. 1057]. This consent that binds the spouses to each other finds its fulfillment in the two "becoming one flesh" [Gen 2:24; cf. Mk 10:8; Eph 5:31]. The consent must be an act of the will of each of the contracting parties, free of coercion or grave external fear. No human power can substitute for this consent.[12]

Before a man and a woman marry, they are free to go their own separate ways. While each is indeed a human person and, as a person, unique and irreplaceable, they have *not* made each other unique, irreplaceable, and nonsubstitutable in their own lives. Before they get married, they may say that they love one another — and they undoubtedly do. Before they marry, they have a special kind of human-friendship love, one that *aspires* to full union, one that *aspires* to marriage and to conjugal love, but they are still at liberty to change their minds and live their own lives independently of one another. They have not yet *established* their uniqueness, their irreplaceability, their nonsubstitutability. But once they have given their irrevocable, personal consent to marriage, they have done something that they cannot undo. For they have, through their own free and self-determining choices, given to themselves and to one another a new kind of identity, and nothing they subsequently do can change this identity. They simply cannot *unspouse* themselves. They cannot make themselves *to be* ex-husbands and ex-wives any more than I can make myself to be an ex-father to the children whom I have begotten. I may be a bad father, a terrible father, but I am still my children's *father.* I may be a bad husband, a terrible husband, but I am still my wife's *husband,* and she is my *wife.* I have made her irreplaceable and nonsubstitutable in my life, and she has made me irreplaceable and nonsubstitutable in hers. We have freely chosen to unite our lives, for better, for worse, for richer, for poorer, in sickness and in health, until *death* do us part.

From this we can see that the *indissolubility* of marriage is

---

[12] *Catechism of the Catholic Church* (San Francisco: Ignatius Press, 1994), nos. 1627–28, p. 406.

ontologically grounded, for it is rooted in the very *being* of the man and the woman, in their freely chosen *identity* as husbands and wives, as persons made irreplaceable and nonsubstitutable in each other's life. The truth that marriage, as a person-affirming reality, is established in and through the free, self-determining choice of the man and the woman is clearly indicated in Scripture. In the second account of the creation of man and of woman, and of marriage, which we find in the second chapter of Genesis, we read that the first man, on awakening from the deep sleep into which God had put him when he fashioned the first woman from his ribs, exclaimed, "This at last is bone of my bones and flesh of my flesh. . . . For this reason a man shall leave father and mother and cleave to his wife, and the two shall become one flesh" (Gen 2:23–24). In a magnificent commentary on this passage, Pope John Paul II makes the following pertinent observation:

> The very formulation of Genesis 2:24 indicates not only that human beings, created as man and woman, were created for unity, but also that precisely *this unity, through which they become "one flesh", has right from the beginning a character of union derived from a choice.* We read, in fact, "a man leaves his father and mother and cleaves to his wife." If the man belongs "by nature" to his father and mother by virtue of procreation, he, on the other hand, "cleaves" by choice to his wife (and she to her husband).[13]

Indeed, it is precisely because marriage, as a person-affirming reality, is rooted in the *irrevocable* choice of the man and the woman *to be* spouses that our Lord not only expressly condemned divorce ("let no man separate what God has joined", Mk 10:9) but also said that any divorce which might possibly take place had no effect whatever on the bond of marriage itself ("whoever divorces his wife and marries another commits adultery against her; and the woman who divorces her husband and marries another commits adultery", Mk 10:11–12).

Thus the *Catechism of the Catholic Church* teaches, "*the marriage*

---

[13] Pope John Paul II, *Original Unity of Man and Woman: Catechesis on Genesis* (Boston: St. Paul Editions, 1981), pp. 81–82 (emphasis added).

bond has been established by God himself. . . . This bond, which results from the free human act of the spouses and their consummation of the marriage, is a reality, henceforth irrevocable, and gives rise to a covenant guaranteed by God's fidelity."[14]

2. Marriage: A Love-enabling Reality

Marriage is not only a person-affirming reality, but it is also a *love-enabling* reality, for it enables husbands and wives to give to one another the unique and special kind of love which we call spousal or conjugal love, one quite different from other kinds of human love. Other kinds of human love—love of neighbor, love of one's children, love of one's enemies—are inclusive, not exclusive. We are to love all our neighbors, all our children, all our enemies. But the love of husband and wife is absolutely unique and different. It is first of all absolutely *exclusive*. A husband can love no other woman as he loves his wife, and a wife can love no other man as she loves her husband. Yet conjugal love, while exclusive, by no means locks husband and wife into an *égoïsme à deux*. To the contrary, it enables them, precisely because of their unique and exclusive love for one another, to love other persons more fully and deeply.

Vatican Council II, in its Pastoral Constitution on the Church in the Modern World, *Gaudium et spes* (nos. 49–50), and Pope Paul VI, in his Encyclical *Humanae vitae* (no. 9), describe conjugal love as a love that is human, total, faithful and exclusive until death, and fecund or fertile. It is, in other words, a love that differs from other kinds of human love because it includes the whole of the other person as a human, sexual, procreative being, sexually complementary in nature. Pope John Paul II, in a magnificent passage in his Apostolic Exhortation *Familiaris consortio*, which the *Catechism of the Catholic Church* makes its own, beautifully describes the nature of this love:

> Conjugal love involves a totality, in which all the elements of the person enter—appeal of the body and instinct, power of

[14] *Catechism of the Catholic Church*, no. 1639, p. 409.

feeling and affectivity, aspiration of the spirit and of the will. It aims at a deeply personal unity, a unity that, beyond union in one flesh, leads to forming one heart and soul; it demands *indissolubility* and *faithfulness* in definitive mutual giving; and it is open to *fertility*.[15]

As Vatican Council II teaches us, marriage is "the intimate community of life and of conjugal love".[16] The institution of marriage *protects and defends* conjugal love, which is the *life-giving* or animating principle of marriage. *Conjugal love, we can rightly say, constitutes the personal reality that the institution of marriage confirms, protects, and sanctions before God and man.*[17] The first act of conjugal love is the act of irrevocable personal consent whereby a man and woman, by freely giving themselves to one another as husband and wife, establish their marriage, a *person-affirming reality*. This person-affirming reality enables husbands and wives to *give* to each other the love that is unique and proper to them, *conjugal love*, because only spouses can give love of this kind and because what makes a man and a woman *to be spouses* is their marriage. Even if this love should, tragically, be actually withdrawn as the spouses' life together unfolds, it remains as the *life-giving principle* and *intrinsic requirement* of marriage. Husbands and wives are under an obligation to *give* this love to each other because they have freely committed themselves to give it; moreover, they *can* give this love because their marriage enables them to do so. Thus a third (3) basic moral criterion for families, which are rooted in

---

[15] Pope John Paul II, *Familiaris consortio*, no. 13; cited in *Catechism of the Catholic Church*, no. 1643, p. 410.

[16] Vatican Council II, *Gaudium et spes*, no. 48.

[17] This is the truth beautifully developed at Vatican Council II in its *Gaudium et spes*, nos. 48–49. Excellent commentaries on these important texts are given by Francisco Gil Hellin and Ramón García de Haro. See Francisco Gil Hellin, "El matrimonio: Amor e institucion", in *Cuestiones fundamentales sobre matrimonio y familia* (II Simposio Internacional de Teologia de la Universidad de Navarra), ed. Augusto Sarmiento et al. (Pamplona: Eunsa, 1980), pp. 231–45, and "El lugar proprio del amor conyugal en la estructura del matrimonio segun la 'Gaudium et spes' ", in *Annales Valentinos* 6, no. 11 (1980): 1–35. See Ramón García de Haro, *Marriage and Family in the Documents of the Magisterium,* trans. from the Italian by William E. May (San Francisco: Ignatius Press, 1993), pp. 234–56.

the reality of marriage, is this: *Husbands and wives must give to each other the gift of conjugal love and deepen it throughout their lives.* By freely consenting to give themselves to one another in marriage, they have established each other as nonsubstitutable and irreplaceable persons and have, by doing so, capacitated themselves to give one another *conjugal love.* This love, "ratified by mutual faith", must be "indissolubly faithful amidst the prosperities and adversities of both body and spirit".[18] Only if they subsequently do what they are now capable of doing will a "civilization of love" be possible.

3. *Marriage: A Life-giving Reality*

This point has already, to some extent, been considered in reflecting on marriage and the generation of human life. Here I will consider this matter from a somewhat different perspective by relating it to conjugal love. Any love between two persons is impossible unless there is some common good that binds them together, and man's capacity for love depends on his willingness to seek a good together with others and to subordinate himself to that good for the sake of others or to others for the sake of that good.

This principle is true of every form of human love and is central to a "civilization of love". But in marriage this principle is revealed in a special and unique way. For in marriage, and in marriage alone, two people, a man and a woman, are united in such a way that they become in a sense "one flesh", that is, the common subject, as it were, of a sexual life. To ensure that one of them does not become for the other nothing more than an object of use, a means to the attainment of some selfish end, they must share the same end or common good. "Such an end, where marriage is concerned"—so Pope John Paul II, writing as the philosopher Karol Wojtyla, has said—"is the procreation and education of children, the future generation, a family, and, at the

---

18 Vatican Council II, *Gaudium et spes,* no. 49.

same time, the continual ripening of the relationship between two people, in all the areas of activity which conjugal life includes. These objective purposes of marriage create in principle the possibility of love and exclude the possibility of treating a person as a means to an end and as an object for use."[19]

In other words, in getting married, a man and a woman not only give to themselves the irrevocable identity of husband and wife but also pledge to one another that they will honor and foster the "goods" or "blessings" of marriage, namely, the procreation and education of children and steadfast faithful love.

The reality of these "goods" is beautifully revealed in the marital or conjugal act, for which marriage also capacitates the spouses. The conjugal act is indeed a very specific and special kind of act.

It is, first of all, an act that manifests uniquely and fittingly the sexual complementarity of husband and wife as male and female. I believe that we can rightly regard human sexuality as *a giving and a receiving*. It is a giving and a receiving for both males and females. However, males and females express their sexuality — their giving and receiving — in complementary ways: the male gives in a receiving sort of way, while the female receives in a giving sort of way. It is not that the male is active and the female passive. There is activity on the part of both, but the man, precisely because of the kind of sexual being that he is, gives in a receiving sort of way while the female, precisely because she is the kind of sexual being she is, receives in a giving sort of way. Their sexuality is, as we shall see more fully in Chapter Two, complementary in this way: male sexuality is an emphasis on giving in a receiving sort of way, whereas female sexuality is an emphasis on receiving in a giving sort of way.

This is illustrated in a striking way in the marital or conjugal act. In this act the husband gives himself to his wife by entering into her body, her person, and in doing so he receives her into himself, while she, in receiving him bodily into herself, gives to him the gift of herself.

[19] Karol Wojtyla, *Love and Responsibility*, p. 30.

To understand the significance of the conjugal or marital act, it is, secondly, most important to recognize that the marital act is not simply a genital act between a man and a woman who "happen" to be married. It is, rather, an act participating in the marriage itself and one made possible only because of the marriage: marriage, in short, *enables* husband and wife to engage in the marital act. I hope now to show why this is true.

Nonmarried men and women are capable of engaging in *genital* acts because they are endowed with genitals. But when nonmarried men and women have sex, they do not, and *cannot, give* themselves to each other and *receive* each other. The man cannot give himself to the woman in a receiving sort of way, nor can she receive him in a giving sort of way. They cannot do so precisely because they are *not* married. They have refused to make each other irreplaceable and nonsubstitutable persons; they have refused to make each other *spouses.* Their sexual act, therefore, does *not* unite two irreplaceable and nonsubstitutable persons; it merely *joins* two individuals who remain in *principle* replaceable, substitutable, disposable. There can be, between them, no true giving or receiving. Their sexual act is, in fact, a lie.[20]

But husbands and wives, who have freely chosen to give themselves the identity of irreplaceable and nonsubstitutable spouses, are capable of the conjugal or spousal act—of giving and receiving. And they are capable of doing so precisely because of their marriage. Thus the conjugal act, precisely as *conjugal,* is an act that participates in their marriage, which, as we have seen, comes into existence when the man gives himself unreservedly to the woman in a receiving sort of way and when she in turn unreservedly receives him in a giving sort of way. The marital act is, therefore, one that respects the "goods" or "blessings" of marriage, that is, the goods of children and of faithful conjugal love. As marital, therefore, it is an act (1) open to the communication of conjugal love and (2) open to the gift of new human life.

If the husband, in choosing to have sex with his wife, refuses to give himself in a receiving sort of way but rather seeks simply to

---

[20] On this, see Pope John Paul II, *Familiaris consortio,* no. 11.

use his wife to satisfy his sexual desires, he is not, in truth, engaging in the conjugal act, nor would his wife be doing so were she to refuse to receive him in a giving sort of way.

A remarkable passage in Pope Paul VI's Encyclical *Humanae vitae* brings out this important truth. In it he said that everyone will recognize that a conjugal act (and here he was using the expression in a purely descriptive sense as a *sexual* act between a man and woman who merely happen to be married and not in its moral sense as an act participating in marriage itself) imposed upon one of the spouses with no consideration of his or her condition or legitimate desires "is not a true act of love" inasmuch as it "opposes what the moral order rightly requires from spouses".[21] It is, in reality, not a true conjugal act, for it violates one of the essential *goods* of marriage, namely, conjugal love, and precisely because it does so it does not inwardly participate in the marriage itself. It is rather an act of spousal abuse.

Indeed, as Pope John Paul II has rightly reminded us, a husband can in a true sense commit adultery with his own wife if he simply uses her as a means to gratify his lust without any concern for her well-being.[22] In saying this, the Holy Father simply reaffirmed the Catholic tradition. After all, a husband can look lustfully at his wife and commit adultery with her in his heart, and if *this* is what he intends in having sex with her, he is committing adultery in the flesh as well. This was the common teaching of the Fathers of the Church and of St. Thomas Aquinas, who said that if a man has intercourse with his wife, not caring that she is his wife but simply a woman whom he can use to satisfy lust, he sins mortally.[23] Marriage does not enable men and women to engage in lustful sexual acts—their sinful hearts do this—but it does enable them to engage in the conjugal or marital act.

Because it participates in the blessings or goods of marriage,

[21] Pope Paul VI, *Humanae vitae*, no. 13.

[22] On this, see Pope John Paul II, *Blessed Are the Pure of Heart: Catechesis on the Sermon of the Mount and Writings of St. Paul* (Boston: St. Paul Editions, 1983), pp. 135–41, esp. pp. 138–41.

[23] On this, see St. Thomas Aquinas, *Summa theologiae*, supplement to pt. 3, q. 49, a. 6.

the conjugal act is also one that is open to the gift of new life. Conjugal love, as we have seen, is a love that is not only human, total, faithful, and exclusive until death, but *fertile*. Conjugal love is procreative in nature. The conjugal act, which uniquely expresses conjugal love, is thus the sort of act meant to welcome new human life, a wondrous and surpassing good. As Jesus said, "Let the little children come to me and do not hinder them" (Lk 18:16).

Hence, just as husbands and wives violate their marriage and render their sexual union *nonmarital* if, in choosing to unite sexually, they deliberately repudiate conjugal love or the unitive meaning of the conjugal act, so too they violate their marriage and render their sexual union *nonmarital* if, in freely choosing to unite sexually, they deliberately repudiate its life-giving or procreative meaning.[24] This brings us to a fourth (4) moral criterion for families: *Spouses ought not, either in anticipation of their marital union, while engaging in it, or during the development of its natural consequences, propose, either as end or means, to impede procreation.*[25] If they choose to do this, they are setting their hearts, their wills, against the good of human life in its transmission. Their choice is anti-life. Moreover, if they do choose to do this, their sexual union is no longer truly a conjugal act, for it is not only anti-life but anti-love — they do not truly "give" themselves unreservedly to one another.[26]

Since the life of a human person must be respected from its beginning, a fifth (5) moral criterion for families immediately ensues, namely, that *It is always gravely wrong freely to choose to abort unborn babies.*

Husbands and wives are to be *responsible* parents, and there can be no true contradiction between their obligation to respect the

---

[24] Pope Paul VI, *Humanae vitae*, no. 13.

[25] This is precisely the definition of contraception found in *Humanae vitae*, no. 14.

[26] For a detailed development of this, see Germain Grisez, John Finnis, Joseph Boyle, and William E. May, " 'Every Marital Act Ought to Be Open to New Life': Toward a Clearer Understanding", in *Thomist* 52 (1988): 365–426; reprinted in the same authors' *The Teaching of "Humanae Vitae": A Defense* (San Francisco: Ignatius Press, 1988). See also Chapters Three and Four below.

procreative good of marriage and the fostering of conjugal love.[27] There may be serious reasons for a married couple to limit the number of their children and perhaps to refrain from having any. But, in exercising their responsibilities in this matter, they ought not freely choose to set their hearts against the good of human life in its transmission; rather, they should freely choose to respect the fertile cycles of the wife.[28] Thus a sixth moral criterion (6) for the family today is this: *Husbands and wives must learn to foster conjugal love by respecting the wife's fertility and by abstaining from the marital act when there is good reason to do so.* Loving husbands and wives are connaturally disposed to honor these criteria and find their violation repugnant. They do so because these criteria naturally flow from the meaning of marriage as a *life-giving reality* rooted in conjugal love, a love open to the good of human life.

4. Marriage: A Sanctifying Reality

The Church has always taught that God is the author of marriage. The creation accounts in the first chapters of Genesis are narratives not only of the creation of the universe, not only the creation of man, male and female, but also of the creation of *marriage*. God is the author, the creator, both of human nature and the nature of marriage. But God is also the one who has willed to enter into a covenant of love with human persons; he is the source of sanctifying grace, which enables us to share his divine nature, just as his only begotten Son, in becoming man, shares our human nature. Nature is for grace; creation is for covenant.

---

[27] Cf. Vatican Council II, *Gaudium et spes*, no. 52.

[28] It is not possible to enter into a discussion of the vast differences between respect for human fertility (natural family planning) and contraception (the free choice to impede procreation) here. However, as Pope John Paul II has rightly noted, there is a "radical difference, both anthropological and moral, between contraception and recourse to the rhythms of the cycle" as ways of regulating conception, a difference ultimately rooted in "irreconcilable concepts of the human person and of human sexuality" (*Familiaris consortio*, no. 32). On this matter, see the article by Grisez et al., referred to in note 26 above.

God has willed our human nature to be the *kind* of nature that it is—the nature of persons endowed with intelligence and free choice—precisely so that we would be free to accept his offer of grace and to enter into an everlasting covenant with him. He cannot give his own life to nonrational creatures likes dogs or cats or chimpanzees, simply because these creatures of his are not inwardly open to receive this surpassing gift. Nor could he become incarnate in creatures of this kind. But he *can* give us his very own life because he has made us to be the kind of beings capable of receiving it. And he *can*—and *has*—become incarnate in human flesh in the person of his only begotten Son, precisely in order to redeem us from sin and enable us to become fully the beings he wills us to be: his own children, his sons and daughters, members of his own divine family.

Similarly, God has given the human reality of marriage the *nature* it has because he wills to integrate it into his divine plan and to make it a means of holiness, of sanctification. And he has so integrated it into his loving and wise plan of human redemption in the life, death, and Resurrection of his Son, who raised the marriages of Christians to the dignity of a sacrament of the new and everlasting covenant.

Recall that the prophets of the Old Testament (Hosea, Jeremiah, Isaiah, Ezekiel) fittingly used the human reality of marriage as a symbol of the loving union or covenant between God and his chosen people. His Son Jesus is the supreme prophet, the One who fully reveals to us the mystery of God's love for mankind, the One who brings into being the new and eternal covenant of God's love for us. And, in the New Testament, Jesus is portrayed as the Bridegroom par excellence, the One who gives his life for his spotless Bride, the Church. Moreover, in the New Testament we read that the human reality of marriage symbolizes the bridal union of Christ and his Church: this is the "great mystery" to which marriage points (cf. Eph 5:23 ff.).

In addition, the marriage of Christians, of those who "marry in the Lord", not only points to or symbolizes the life-giving, love-giving, grace-giving, and sanctifying union of Christ and the Church, but it also inwardly participates in this bridal union and makes it efficaciously present in the world. Christians have already, by baptism, become "new" creatures in Christ: they have become, through Christ, with Christ, and in Christ, members of the divine family, children of his Father, led by his Spirit. As a result, when Christians unite sexually with others, they do so, not as isolated individuals, but as members of Christ's living Body, the Church. Should they do so outside of marriage, they not only act immorally but desecrate the Body of Christ (cf. 1 Cor 6:15–17). But when they give themselves to each other in marriage, which is to be honored in every way (cf. Heb 13:4), they marry "in the Lord". Precisely because Christian husbands and wives are *already,* through baptism, "new" creatures, members of the household of God, their marital union inwardly participates in the grace-giving, sanctifying, redemptive union of Christ and his Church. Their marriage is a sacrament of sanctifying grace.

Thus the marriage of Christians is a sanctifying reality. It enables Christian husbands and wives to love one another with a redemptive, sanctifying love, for their human conjugal love has been graced by Christ himself and merges the divine with the human. In forming a communion of persons, Christian husbands and wives indeed bring into existence the "domestic Church", the "Church in miniature".[29] The Christian family, therefore, has a specific and original role to play within the larger Church. Its mission is to participate in a unique way in the redemptive work of Christ. Its task, as Pope John Paul II has so well expressed it, is to be fully what it *is,* that is, a believing and evangelizing community, a community in dialogue with God, a community serving others by transforming the world through Christ's redemptive love. It is a community that participates in the prophetic, priestly, and kingly mission of Christ.[30]

Marriage, by the will of God, has been made a sacrament of

[29] On this, see Vatican Council II, *Lumen gentium* [Dogmatic Constitution on the Church], no. 11; *Apostolicam actuositatem* [Decree on the Lay Apostolate], no. 11; Pope John Paul II, *Familiaris consortio,* no. 49; *Catechism of the Catholic Church,* nos. 1655–58, pp. 413–14.

[30] On this, see Pope John Paul II, *Familiaris consortio,* nos. 49–64; see also his *Letter to Families.*

sanctifying grace, capable of helping Christian husbands and wives answer God's call to be holy, enabling them to participate in a unique and indispensable way in the redemptive work of Christ. Thus a seventh (7) criterion for the Christian family today is this: *The Christian family must carry out its mission as the domestic Church and participate in Christ's redemptive work.* This is a subject that will be explored in greater depth in Chapter Five.

Marriage and Family as Serving Life and the Human Community

I. *Parents' Obligations toward Their Children*

Husbands and wives are called not only to receive life lovingly but to nourish it humanely and to educate it in the love and service of God, and their marriage *capacitates* them for these tasks too. This is an eighth (8) moral criterion of the family: *Parents have the duty, and the right, to educate their own children.* This duty and the right corresponding to it flow from the very nature of fatherly and motherly love, a love that is fulfilled "in the task of education as it completes and perfects its service to life".[31]

The duty of parents to educate their children encompasses the following elements. First of all, parents (a) need to help their children acquire a sense of values, in particular a correct attitude toward material goods, which are intended to serve *persons,* who must always be considered as more precious for what they *are* than for what they *have.* Second (b), they must help their children learn that they must cultivate virtues if they are to be truly the persons they are meant to be, and particularly today, in a world

---

[31] Pope John Paul II, *Familiaris consortio,* no. 36. See also *Catechism of the Catholic Church,* no. 1653, p. 412, where we read: "The fruitfulness of conjugal love extends to the fruits of the moral, spiritual, and supernatural life that parents hand on to their children by education. Parents are the principal and first educators of their children. In this sense the fundamental task of marriage and family is to be at the service of life."

that is hostile to the "civilization of love", the virtues of justice and love. Finally (c), they need to educate their children in the area of human sexuality, leading them to appreciate the beauty of their sexuality and the human significance of and need for the virtue of chastity, a virtue that enables them to come into possession of their sexual desires and urges and not to be possessed by them, a virtue that capacitates them to *give themselves away in love to others.*[32]

The work of parents in educating their own children is indispensable. "It is not an exaggeration", Pope John Paul II has said, "to reaffirm that the life of nations, of states, and of international organizations 'passes' through the family. . . . [Indeed] *through the family passes the primary current of the civilization of love,* which finds therein its "social foundations'."[33] Parents share their educational mission with other individuals or institutions, such as the Church and the State. But it is imperative that the mission of education respect the *principle of subsidiarity.* This implies the legitimacy and, indeed, the need of giving help to parents, but it is limited by their right as *the primary educators* of their children. Indeed "all other participants in the process of education are only able to carry out their responsibilities *in the name of the parents, with their consent,* and, to a certain degree, *with their authorization."*[34] Thus a ninth (9) criterion for the family today is this: *Church and State must both honor the primary right of parents as educators of their children and cooperate with them in this educative task.*

Children learn from the example given to them perhaps even more than from what is said to them. Thus, in connection with the right and duty of parents to educate their children, it seems to me that the following is sound advice: one of the best gifts that a husband can give his wife is to love her children and, vice versa, one of the best gifts a wife can give her husband is to love his children. And one of the best gifts a father can give his children is to love their mother, and vice versa.

---

[32] On this, see *Familiaris consortio,* no. 37.
[33] Pope John Paul II, *Letter to Families,* no. 15.
[34] Ibid., no. 16.

2. The Family's Service to Society

By nature and vocation the family rooted in the marriage of one man and one woman is open to other families and to society. The obligation of the family to serve society and the wider human community is, indeed, not something added on to or extrinsic to the family, but is rooted in its *being*.

> The family has vital and organic links with society, since it is its foundation and nourishes it continually through its service to life; it is from the family that citizens come to birth and it is within the family that they find the first school of the social virtues that are the animating principle of the existence and development of society itself.[35]

The "first and fundamental contribution" of the family to society is "the very experience of communion and sharing that should characterize the family's daily life".[36] By becoming what it is meant to be, the family is the first and most efficacious school of socialization, through the spontaneous gratuity of the relationships among its members, which takes place through their cordial welcoming of each other, their disinterested availability, their generous service, their deep solidarity.

The family contributes to the good of society by works of social service, especially by means of hospitality, by opening "the door of one's home and still more of one's heart to the pleas of one's brothers and sisters".[37]

A tenth (10) criterion of the family today, therefore, is the following: *The family must serve society by works of social service, in particular, by hospitality to others.*

Precisely because the family is the first school in the "civilization of love" and contributes so efficaciously to the well-being of society, there is a corresponding obligation on the part of society and the State to recognize and respect the role of the family in the

---

[35] Pope John Paul II, *Familiaris consortio*, no. 42. See also *Catechism of the Catholic Church*, no. 2207.

[36] Ibid.

[37] Ibid., no. 44.

development of society. Thus an eleventh (11) criterion of the family of today is this: *Society and the State must serve the family: they must make it possible for it to obtain the helps of which it has need and recognize the rights of the family in a formal way.*[38]

Since, unfortunately, the rights of the family are today threatened and ignored by many states and societies, families themselves "must be the first to take steps to see that laws and institutions of the state not only do not offend but support and positively defend the rights and duties of families".[39] Families must become protagonists of "family politics" and assume "responsibility for transforming society". This gives us a twelfth (12) criterion for the family of today: *Families must defend their rights and duties.*

In connection with this matter, there is great need today to respect the rights of women and, in particular, of mothers. There is, of course, "no doubt that the equal dignity and responsibility of men and women fully justifies women's access to public functions". Nonetheless,

> while it must be recognized that women have the same right as men to perform various public functions, society must be structured in such a way that wives and mothers are *not in practice compelled* to work outside the home, and that their families can live and prosper in a dignified way even when they themselves devote their full time to their own family. . . . The mentality which honors women more for their work outside the home than for their work within the family must be overcome. This requires that men should truly esteem and love women with total respect for their personal dignity, and that society should create and develop conditions favoring work in the home.[40]

A thirteenth (13) criterion for the family today, therefore, can be put as follows: *Society must respect the contribution made by mothers*

---

[38] On this, cf. ibid., no. 44. See also the *Charter of the Rights of the Family presented by the Holy See to All Persons, Institutions and Authorities Concerned with the Mission of the Family in Today's World,* October 23, 1983. See also *Catechism of the Catholic Church,* nos. 2210–11, pp. 533–34.

[39] Pope John Paul II, *Familiaris consortio,* no. 44.

[40] Ibid., no. 23.

who choose to remain at home and care for their children and secure its just compensation.

Conclusion: The Family and Society

My fundamental argument has been that the human race survives only in its children; and its children can flourish fully only in the family rooted in the marriage of one man and woman. Only if this truth is recognized can a "civilization of love" be developed.

But today this understanding of the family is under attack. According to the champions of "free sex", of utilitarianism and individualism, of militant feminism and the "gay" revolution, a family is essentially a matter of choice. According to those advocating these ideas, the "family" should be redefined so as to emphasize bonds formed, not so much by marriage and kinship, as by personal choices and declared commitment.[41] In other words, "family" ought to be defined primarily in terms of the free choices made by the individuals who form them—and who are free to leave them whenever they are so disposed.

This is folly. As we have seen, the future of the human race passes through the family rooted in the marriage of one man and one woman. Children *need* both a mother and a father. Mothering does not present the difficulties that fathering does. As one writer notes, "simply stated, an adult female will be naturally transformed into a social mother when she bears a child, but there is no corresponding natural transformation for a male."[42] The father-involved family, as another author points out, "is a fragile cultural achievement that cannot be taken for granted".[43]

The essence of the matter can be put this way: In order for a male to be induced to undertake the responsibility of fathering, he

[41] See, for instance, Carol Levine, "AIDS and Changing Concepts of the Family", *Milbank Quarterly* 68, supplement 1 (1990): 36–37.

[42] Peter Wilson, *Man the Promising Primate: The Conditions of Human Evolution,* 2d ed. (New Haven: Yale University Press, 1983), p. 71.

[43] John W. Miller, *Biblical Faith and Fathering: Why We Call God "Father"* (New York: Paulist Press, 1989), p. 5.

needs, first of all, to give himself unreservedly to a particular woman, who in turn must receive him and, in receiving him, give herself to him. Both the man and the woman, if the father's role is to be properly fulfilled, must give themselves to each other unreservedly. They must, in other words, take upon themselves the responsibility of marriage, of fidelity to each other, of selfless service to their children, of building a "civilization of love". Consequently, as John W. Miller has so eloquently put it, when

> a culture ceases to support, through its mores, symbols, models, laws, and rituals, the sanctity of the sexual bond between a man and his wife and a father's involvement with his own children, powerful natural forces will inevitably take over in favor of the mother-alone family; the fragility of the sexual bond (and the investment of fathers with children) will give way to the strength of the primary bond between mother and child.[44]

This enables us to formulate a fourteenth (14) criterion for families today: *Society must support the sanctity of the marriage bond if men are to be fathers to their children.*

A slogan voiced by champions of "free love", utilitarianism, and individualism is that "no unwanted child ought ever to be born." This is banal. Opposed to it is a truth rooted in the reality of human existence, namely, that "no person, including children, ought to be unwanted." The only way to develop a society in which all human persons, including unborn children, are indeed loved and wanted is to respect the beauty of a family rooted in the marriage of one man and one woman. Only by doing so can the "civilization of love" become a reality.

---

[44]Ibid., p. 19. The text is italicized in the original. See also George Gilder, *Men and Marriage* (Gretna, LA: Pelican, 1986) and Blankenhorn, especially pp. 201–34.

2

Marriage and the Complementarity of Male and Female

The "Beatifying Beginning" of Human Existence

It is fitting to begin our investigation into marriage and the complementarity of male and female with the first two chapters of Genesis. It is fitting to do so because these chapters, which contain the stories of what Pope John Paul II has called the "beatifying beginning of human existence",[1] set forth precious truths about men and women of utmost importance to our topic.

The narrative found in the first chapter of Genesis, attributed to the Priestly tradition, declares:

> God created man [*ha 'adam*] in his image; in the divine image he created him; male and female he created them. God blessed them, saying: "Be fertile and multiply; fill the earth and subdue it. Have dominion over the fish of the sea, the birds of the air, and all the living things that move on the earth" (Gen 1:27–28).

In the second chapter of Genesis, attributed to the Yahwist source, we find the following:

---

[1] See Pope John Paul II, "Nuptial Meaning of the Body", General Audience of January 9, 1980, in *Original Unity of Man and Woman: Catechesis on the Book of Genesis* (Boston: St. Paul Editions, 1981), p. 108. In this text, Pope John Paul II is explicitly concerned with the account in Genesis 2, but the expression "beatifying beginning" can also be applied to the narrative in Genesis 1.

The Lord God formed man [ha 'adam] out of the clay of the ground and blew into his nostrils the breath of life, and so man became a living being.... The Lord God said: "It is not good for the man [ha 'adam] to be alone. I will make a suitable partner for him."... The Lord God cast a deep sleep on the man, and while he was asleep, he took out one of his ribs and closed up its place with flesh. The Lord God then built up into a woman [ishah] the rib that he had taken from the man [ha 'adam]. When he brought her to the man [ha 'adam], the man [ha 'adam] said: "This one, at last, is bone of my bones and flesh of my flesh; this one shall be called 'woman' [ishah], for out of 'her man' [ish] this one has been taken." That is why a man [ish] leaves his father and mother and clings to his wife [ishah], and the two of them become one body. The man [ish] and his wife [ishah] were both naked, yet they felt no shame (Gen 2:7, 18, 21–25).

In my opinion, three crucial truths about men and women, marriage, and the complementarity of the sexes are rooted in these texts: (1) that men and women are equally persons; (2) that God is the author of marriage, the one who gives to it its defining characteristics; and (3) that men and women are body-persons, not spirit-persons.

1. *The personhood of man and woman.* That both man and woman are equally persons is luminously expressed in Genesis 1, even though it does not use the term *person.* But the text makes it clear that human beings, male and female, are persons, for it affirms that "God created man [ha 'adam] in his image; in the divine image he created him, male and female he created them" (Gen 1:27). Note that the Hebrew word *adam* is not used here as a proper name for the first human male, as it was in later texts of Genesis, but rather as the generic term to designate man, a human being, whether male or female. Being created in the image of God, man, male and female, is a person, that is, a being endowed with intellect and will, with the capacity to come to know the truth, to make free choices, and by so doing to be self-determining. Both the man and the woman are thus persons, the sort of beings

toward whom "the only proper and adequate attitude", as Karol Wojtyla has said, "is love."[2] And to these human persons, made in his image, to the woman as well as to the man, God gave dominion over the earth and the nonhuman creatures inhabiting it, its waters, and its atmosphere.

The truth that woman, like man, is a person is expressed more poetically in Genesis 2. There the man, who is initially identified by the generic term for human being, *adam*, is created first. But it is "not good" for him to be alone. The other living creatures of the earth, however, are not equal to him; they are not worthy to be his companion, his partner. Thus the Lord God, after casting the man into a deep sleep, forms from his rib a woman so that there can be a creature noble enough to be his partner, to share life with him. And, on awakening from his sleep, the man delights in finding this partner, this "bone of his bones and the flesh of his flesh", and in his delight gives to her the name *ishah*, "woman", and to himself the name *ish*, "man". Both are obviously regarded, in this text, as equal in their dignity, a dignity far surpassing that of the other living creatures God has made.

In addition, if we reflect on these Genesis passages in the light of revelation, we realize that God, who created man and woman, is a God who is love and who, in himself, "lives a mystery of personal loving communion" in a Trinity of persons. It thus follows that by creating man and woman in his own image, by making them *persons*, "God inscribed into the humanity of man and woman the vocation, and thus the capacity and responsibility of love and communion."[3]

[2] Karol Wojtyla, *Love and Responsibility*, trans. H. T. Willetts (New York: Farrar, Straus, and Giroux, 1981; reprinted, San Francisco: Ignatius Press, 1993), p. 41.

[3] Pope John Paul II, Apostolic Exhortation *Familiaris consortio*, no. 11. All men and women are called to love and communion. As the Holy Father notes later in this same passage, "Christian revelation recognizes two specific ways of realizing the vocation of the human person, in its entirety, to love: marriage and virginity or celibacy. Either one is in its own proper form an actuation of the most profound truth of man, of his being 'created in the image of God'."

Some men and women freely choose celibacy in order to give themselves more fully to the service of our Lord and his people. Others, who may earnestly long to marry, accept celibacy because for one reason or another it is not possible for them

2. *God is the author of marriage.* A second major feature of these texts is that they are accounts not only of the origin of the human race, male and female, but also of the origin of marriage. They proclaim that God is the author of marriage, the one who gives to it its "defining characteristics".[4] Indeed, it is to both these passages of Genesis that Jesus later referred when, in responding to the Pharisees' question about divorce and in replying that it was only because of the "hardness" of men's hearts that Moses had permitted divorce, he insisted that divorce was not God's will, for "At the beginning of creation God made them male and female [Gen 1:27]; for this reason a man shall leave his father and mother and the two shall become as one [Gen 2:24]. They are no longer two but one flesh. Therefore," he concluded, "let no man separate what God has joined" (Mk 10:6–9).

What are these "defining characteristics" of marriage? A central one is that marriage is an intimate, personal union between one man and one woman in which they "become one body, one flesh". By giving themselves to one another in marriage, a man and a woman actualize their vocation to love and to enter into a communion of persons.

Here it is important to note that the text of Genesis 2 clearly indicates that the reality of marriage comes to be when a man and a woman "give" themselves to one another by an act of irrevo-

---

to marry. For such men and women the requirements of the truth—of God's reign—impose a "situational celibacy". On this, see the observations of Edward Schillebeeckx, O.P., *Marriage: Human Reality and Saving Mystery* (New York: Sheed & Ward, 1965), p. 120; see also Roger Balducelli, O.S.F.S., "The Decision for Celibacy", *Theological Studies* 36 (1975): 219–42.

[4] Schillebeeckx, p. 24: "To be created by God, or to be named by him, implied a commission to serve him. The whole of the Old Testament ethic of marriage and family was based on this. The things of the earth and man received their *hoq* or *huqqah* [their statutes of limitation, their defining characteristics] with their creation; each received, on creation, its intrinsic conditions of existence, its defined limits." That God is the author of marriage has always been affirmed by the Magisterium of the Church. See, for example, Council of Trent, DS 1797; Pope Pius XI, Encyclical *Casti connubii*, DS 3700; Vatican Council II, *Gaudium et spes* [Pastoral Constitution on the Church in the Modern World], no. 48.

cable personal choice. Pope John Paul II brings this out in commenting on Genesis 2:24:

> The very formulation of Genesis 2:24 indicates not only that human beings, created as man and woman, were created for unity, but also that precisely *this unity, through which they become "one flesh", has right from the beginning a character of union derived from a choice.* We read, in fact, that "a man leaves his father and mother and cleaves to his wife." If the man belongs "by nature" to his father and mother by virtue of procreation, he, on the other hand, "cleaves" by choice to his wife (and she to her husband).[5]

The act of marital consent is an act of choice, whereby the man chooses this particular woman as the irreplaceable and nonsubstitutable person with whom he wills to share his life henceforward until death and whereby the woman in turn chooses this particular man as the irreplaceable and nonsubstitutable person with whom she wills to share her life henceforward until death. Marriage is, therefore, the intimate partnership of life and love between man and woman, brought into being by their own act of irrevocable personal consent.

Another "defining characteristic" of marriage is set forth in Genesis 1, where the man and the woman—the husband and wife—are blessed and commanded to "be fertile and multiply" (Gen 1:28). This text shows that marriage and the intimate partnership of love and life that it establishes between man and woman is ordered to the procreation and education of children.[6] Inasmuch as the union of man and woman in marriage is dynamically oriented to the generation of new human life, we can see one of

[5] Pope John Paul II, "Marriage Is One and Indissoluble in the First Chapters of Genesis", General Audience of November 21, 1979, in *Original Unity of Man and Woman*, pp. 81–82.

[6] On this, see Vatican Council II, *Gaudium et spes*, no. 48: "By its very nature the institution of marriage and married love is ordered to the procreation and education of the offspring and it is in them that it finds its crowning glory." See also no. 50: "Marriage and married love are by nature ordered to the procreation and education of children. Indeed, children are the supreme gift of marriage and greatly contribute to the good of the parents themselves."

the reasons why God created man in two differing but complementary sexes, male and female. The human race is sexually differentiated into male and female because it must be so if it is to survive. A man cannot generate new human life with another man, nor can a woman do so with another woman. In generating human life, man and woman do indeed "complement" one another. Fertility, we need to keep in mind, is a blessing from God, and it requires the complementary fertility of husband and wife. One biblical scholar, commenting on this passage, has appropriately observed that "Progeny is a gift from God, the fruit of his blessing. Progeny are conceived because of the divine power which has been transferred to men." And, he continues, "[T]he blessing . . . indicates that fertility is the purpose of the sexual distinction, albeit not the exclusive purpose of this distinction."[7]

3. *Men and women are body-persons, not spirit-persons.* A third critically important feature of these texts is that they characterize human persons, male and female, as *bodily beings.* The account in Genesis 1 describes them as living beings who are bodily and sexual in nature, blessed with fertility and summoned to multiply their kind. Genesis 2 is even more graphic in showing the bodily character of the human beings whom God, as Genesis 1 instructs us, created in his own image. For Genesis 2 shows that man

> is constituted by two principles, one low ("dust of the earth"), one high ("breath of life"). The human being first comes to sight as a formed and animated (or breathing) dust of the ground. Higher than the earth, yet still bound to it, the human being has a name, *adam* (from *adamah,* meaning "earth" or "ground"), which reminds him of his lowly terrestrial origins. Man is, from the start, up from below and in between.[8]

Moreover, it is clear from Genesis 2 that the human body is personal in nature and that it reveals or discloses the person. For

---

[7] Raymond Collins, "The Bible and Sexuality I", *Biblical Theology Bulletin* 7 (1977): 156.

[8] Leon Kass, "Man and Woman: An Old Story", *First Things: A Monthly Journal of Religion and Public Life* 17 (November 1991): 16.

"the man", on awakening from the deep sleep into which the Lord God had cast him and on seeing "the woman" who had been formed from his rib, declares: "This one, at last, is bone of my bones and flesh of my flesh." In uttering this cry, the man, as Pope John Paul II has noted, "seems to say: here is *a body that expresses the 'person'!*"[9] Men and women, in other words, are persons, but they are not spirits or disembodied minds. When God created man he did not, as some dualistic-minded theologians today think, create "an isolated subjectivity . . . who experiences existence in [either] a female body-structure . . . [or] a male body-structure."[10] Quite to the contrary, God, in creating *human* persons, created persons who are bodily in nature.

This is a matter of utmost importance. Human persons are bodily, sexual beings. Their sexuality, "by means of which man and woman give themselves to one another through the acts mutual and exclusive to spouses, is by no means something merely biological, but concerns the innermost being of the human person as such",[11] and it does so because human sexuality is the sexuality of a human person and is hence personal in character. Sexuality has to do with our bodiliness. Our bodies, however, are not impersonal instruments that are to be used *by* our persons; instead, they are integral components of our *being* as *persons.* From this it follows that the more apparent anatomical differences between males and females are, as one contemporary writer puts it, "not mere accidentals or mere attachments . . . [instead], differences in the body are *revelations* of differences in the depths of their being."[12]

[9] Pope John Paul II, "Nuptial Meaning of the Body", p. 109.

[10] On this, see Anthony Kosnik et al., *Human Sexuality: New Directions in American Catholic Thought.* A Study Commissioned by The Catholic Theological Society of America (New York: Paulist Press, 1977), pp. 83–84. An excellent critique of the dualism underlying much contemporary thought, including that of influential Catholic theologians, is provided by Germain Grisez, "Dualism and the New Morality", in *Atti del Congresso internazionale (Roma-Napoli, 17–24 aprile 1974): Tommaso d'Aquino nel suo settimo centenario,* vol. 5, *L'agire morale,* ed. M. Zalba (Napoli: Edizioni Domenicane Napoli, 1977).

[11] Pope John Paul II, *Familiaris consortio,* no. 11.

[12] Robert E. Joyce, in Mary Rosera Joyce and Robert E. Joyce, *New Dynamics in Sexual Love* (Collegeville, MN: St. John's University Press, 1970), pp. 34–35.

The human body, in other words, is a revelation of a human person; and since the human body is inescapably either male or female, it is the revelation of a man-person or a woman-person. Precisely because of their sexual differences, manifest in their bodies, the man-person and the woman-person can give themselves to one another bodily. Moreover, since the body, male or female, is the expression of a human person, a man and a woman, in giving their bodies to one another, give their *persons* to one another. The bodily gift of a man and a woman to each other is the outward sign, the sacrament, of the *communion of persons* existing between them. And this sacrament, in turn, is an image of the communion of persons in the Trinity. The body, therefore, is the means and the sign of the gift of the man-person to the woman-person. Pope John Paul II calls this capacity of the body to express the communion of persons the *nuptial meaning of the body*.[13] It is precisely for this reason that genital coition outside of marriage is gravely immoral. When unmarried individuals have sex, the sex act does not unite two irreplaceable and nonsubstitutable persons but rather joins two individuals who are in principle disposable, replaceable, and substitutable. But when husband and wife give themselves to one another in the marital act, they do so as irreplaceable and nonsubstitutable spouses. Pope John Paul II has expressed this truth eloquently:

> The total physical self-giving would be a lie if it were not the sign and fruit of a total personal self-giving, in which the whole person, including the temporal dimension, is present.... The only "place" in which this self-giving in its whole truth is made possible is marriage, the covenant of conjugal love freely

---

[13] The "nuptial meaning" of the body is developed in many of the addresses of Pope John Paul II on the "theology of the body". See in particular, "Nuptial Meaning of the Body", pp. 106–12; "The Man-Person Becomes a Gift in the Freedom of Love", General Audience of January 16, 1980, in ibid., pp. 113–20; and "Mystery of Man's Original Innocence", General Audience of January 30, 1980, in ibid., pp. 121–27. An excellent introduction to the thought of Pope John Paul II on this matter is provided by Richard M. Hogan, "A Theology of the Body: A Commentary on the Audiences of Pope John Paul II from September 5, 1979 to May 6, 1981", in *Fidelity* 1, no. 1 (December 1981): 10–15, 24–27.

and consciously chosen, whereby man and woman accept the intimate community of life and love willed by God himself, which only in this light manifests its true meaning.[14]

Our examination of the Genesis texts has shown us that man and woman are equally persons, that God has made them for each other, and that they are complementary in their sexuality. But the nature of their sexual complementarity needs to be set forth in more detail. It is evident that their sexual complementarity is intimately related to their vocation to marriage and parenthood. Indeed, as the *Catechism of the Catholic Church* teaches, "everyone, man and woman, should acknowledge and accept his sexual *identity*. Physical, moral, and spiritual *difference* and *complementarity* are oriented toward the goods of marriage and the flourishing of family life."[15] Husbands and wives, as we have seen in examining the "defining characteristics" of marriage, have the high vocation, the *munus* or noble responsibility, to cooperate with God in handing on human life and in giving to new human life the home where it can take root and grow.[16] Not all men and women, of course, become husbands and wives, fathers and mothers. Yet all men are potentially fathers and all women are potentially mothers. Even if they do not generate children, as men and women they are called upon to exercise analogously a kind of spiritual fatherhood and spiritual motherhood in the living out of their lives.

I will now endeavor to express more specifically the complementarity of male and female. I will begin by reflecting on the act which is "proper and exclusive to spouses",[17] namely, the marital act.

---

[14] Pope John Paul II, *Familiaris consortio*, no. 11.

[15] *Catechism of the Catholic Church*, no. 2333, p. 560.

[16] A rich analysis of the Latin term *munus*, used in many magisterial texts to designate the vocation to parenthood, is provided by Janet Smith. See her *Humanae Vitae: A Generation Later* (Washington, DC: The Catholic University of America Press, 1991), esp. pp. 136–48. See also her "The *Munus* of Transmitting Human Life: A New Approach to *Humanae Vitae*", *Thomist* 54 (July 1990): 385–427.

[17] Pope John Paul II, *Familiaris consortio*, no. 11.

The Marital Act as Expressing and Symbolizing the Complementarity of Male and Female

A man and a woman become husband and wife when they give themselves to each other in and through the act of irrevocable personal consent that makes them to *be* spouses. They become literally "one flesh", "one body", when they consummate their marriage and give themselves to each other in the act proper and exclusive to them as spouses, the spousal or the marital act. In this act they come intimately to "know"[18] each other in an unforgettable way, and to know each other precisely as male and female.

The marital act is a unique kind of act. It is the personal act of two subjects, husband and wife. In it they "give" themselves to one another and "receive" one another. Yet they do so in strikingly different and complementary ways, for it is an act made possible precisely by reason of their sexual differences. The wife does not have a penis; therefore, in this act of marital union she cannot enter the body, the person, of her husband, whereas he can and does personally enter into her body-person. He gives himself to her, and by doing so he receives her. On the other hand, she is uniquely capable of receiving her husband personally into her body, her self, and in so doing she gives herself to him. The wife's receiving of her husband in a giving sort of way is just as essential to the unique meaning of this act as is her husband's giving of himself to her in a receiving sort of way. The husband cannot, in this act, give himself to his wife unless she gives herself to him by receiving him, nor can she receive him in this self-giving way unless he gives himself to her in this receiving way.[19] As the philosopher Robert Joyce says, "the man does not force himself

---

[18] "Adam *knew* Eve his wife, and she conceived and bore Cain, saying: 'I have begotten a man with the help of the Lord' " (Gen 4:1).

[19] When nonmarried males and females engage in sexual coition, they do not "give" themselves to each other or "receive" each other. Their act in no way expresses and symbolizes personal union precisely because they have refused to give and receive each other unconditionally as persons. In genital union, such individuals do not make a "gift" of themselves to each other; rather, they use each other as means to attain subjectively determined ends.

upon the woman, but gives himself in a receiving manner. The woman does not simply submit herself to the man, but receives him in a giving manner."[20] Note that in the marital act the husband is not active and the wife passive. Each is active but is active in differing and complementary ways.

In giving himself to his wife in the marital act, moreover, the husband releases into her body-person millions of his sperm, which go in search for an ovum. Should his wife indeed be fertile and an ovum present within her, one of the sperm may succeed in uniting with it, in becoming "one flesh" with it, and in doing so bring into existence a new human person. These facts dramatically illumine another dimension or aspect of the male-female sexual complementarity. The man, as it were, symbolizes the superabundance and differentiation of being, for his sperm are differentiated into those that will generate a male child and those that will generate a female child. The woman, as it were, symbolizes the oneness or unity of being (insofar as she ordinarily produces only one ovum) and what we might call the withinness or abidingness of being.[21]

In reflecting on the significance of the marital act, we can also say, I believe, that the man, the husband, is the one who emphasizes, in giving himself wholeheartedly to his wife, an outgoing, productive kind of joyful existence, while the woman, the wife, is the one who emphasizes, in receiving her husband wholeheartedly into her person, the abidingness and peaceful tranquillity of existence.

---

[20] Robert E. Joyce, *Human Sexual Ecology: A Philosophy and Ethics of Man and Woman* (Washington, DC: University Press of America, 1980), pp. 70–71.

[21] On this, see Joyce, ibid., pp. 70–71: "The man emphasizes in his way the giving power of being and the *otherness* of every being in the universe. . . . The man emphasizes (with his sperm production) manyness, differentiation, and plurality . . . characteristics based on uniqueness and otherness." The woman, on the other hand, "emphasizes . . . the receiving power of her being and the *withinness* of every being in the universe. . . . The woman emphasizes (with her ova production) oneness and sameness . . . characteristics based on withinness and superrelatedness."

"Defining" Man and Woman, Male and Female

What this analysis of the marital act suggests is that human sexuality is a giving and a receiving, a superabundant, outgoing otherness and a peaceful, rest-bringing withinness. By virtue of their sexuality—which, we must remember, is not something merely biological but something that "concerns the innermost being of the human person"—men and women are summoned to give themselves to others and to receive them, and to do so in a unique and exclusive way in marriage. They are likewise summoned to be outgoing and superabundant in their giving and to bring others peace and rest by receiving them within themselves. But men and women, males and females, give superabundantly and receive in peaceful tranquillity in strikingly different modalities.

Human sexuality, in other words, is realized differently in male and female, in man and woman. Male sexuality emphasizes giving in a receiving sort of way and the superabundant plenitude and otherness of being; female sexuality emphasizes receiving in a giving sort of way and the peace-giving, rest-bringing withinness of being. It therefore seems to me that Joyce's way of "defining" man and woman is correct. He does so as follows:

> I would define a man as a human being who both gives in a receiving way and receives in a giving way, but is so structured in his being that he is emphatically inclined toward giving in a receiving way. The nature of being a man is an emphasis on giving in a receiving way. A woman is a human being who both gives in a receiving way and receives in a giving way, but is so structured in her being that she is emphatically inclined toward receiving in a giving way. The nature of being a woman is an emphasis on receiving in a giving way.... The sexuality of man and woman ... is orientated in opposite but very complementary ways.[22]

---

[22] Ibid., pp. 67–69. This way of expressing the complementary character of male and female sexuality and of man and woman may seem, on the surface, to conflict with some things that Pope John Paul II has said. For instance, in his General Audience of February 6, 1980, "Man and Woman: A Mutual Gift for Each Other", the Holy Father, commenting on the text of Genesis 2, observed: "It seems that the

Moreover, as we have seen, the man emphasizes in his being the superabundant otherness or plenitude of being, whereas the woman emphasizes its withinness and abidingness, its capacity to bring rest and peace. Man and woman, we must remember, are made in the image of God. They are two differing and complementary ways of imaging him. He is both the superabundant giver of good gifts and the One who is ever within us, who is with us and for us, and who longs to welcome us and to give our hearts refreshment and peace. He is, as the beautiful hymn of Henry Van Dyck expresses it, both the "Wellspring of the joy of living" and the "Ocean depth of happy rest".[23] Both man and woman are to image God in his superabundant goodness and his peaceful immanence, to image him as the "wellspring of the joy of living" and "ocean depth of happy rest". But the man, in imaging God,

---

second narrative of creation has assigned to man 'from the beginning' the function of the one who, above all, *receives* the gift [of the woman]. 'From the beginning' the woman is entrusted to his eyes, to his consciousness, to his sensitivity, to his 'heart'. He, on the other hand, must, in a way, ensure the same process of the exchange of the gift, the mutual interpenetration of giving and receiving as a gift, which, precisely through its reciprocity, creates a real communion of persons" (in *Original Unity of Man and Woman*, p. 133). This would seem to imply that male sexuality is a receiving in a giving way and female sexuality is a giving in a receiving way.

I do not, however, think that there is any real opposition between Joyce's way of expressing the male-female difference and what Pope John Paul II says here. Genesis 2 certainly portrays the woman as God's wonderful gift to the man, to whom she is entrusted and who is to receive her lovingly. But neither Genesis 2 nor Pope John Paul II is here concerned with the precise *modality* whereby the man is to "receive" the woman and "give" himself to her and vice versa. The man, in fact, "receives" the woman given to him by God by taking the initiative, giving himself to her and giving to her her name in his poetic cry: "This one at last is bone of my bones and flesh of my flesh; this one shall be called 'woman,' for out of 'her man' has she been taken"—the "biblical prototype", as Pope John Paul II has noted elsewhere, of the Song of Songs [in "By the Communion of Persons Man Becomes the Image of God", General Audience of November 14, 1979, in *Original Unity of Man and Woman*, p. 71]. God presents the woman to the man as a gift that he is to welcome lovingly; but the man, in his cry of joy on seeing this woman, surrenders or gives himself to her and, by doing so, receives the woman "entrusted to his eyes, to his consciousness, to his sensitivity, to his 'heart' ".

[23] Henry Van Dyck, "Joyful, Joyful, We Adore Thee", *Poems of Henry Van Dyck* (New York: Charles Scribner's Sons, n.d.). This beautiful hymn has been set to music, using as the musical score Beethoven's Ninth Symphony.

emphasizes his transcendent, superabundant goodness, his glory as the "wellspring of the joy of living", while the woman, in imaging God, emphasizes his immanence, his "withinness," his glory as the "ocean depth of happy rest".

The man, like the woman, is summoned to receive as well as to give, to be an "ocean depth of happy rest" as well as a "wellspring of the joy of living"; the woman, like the man, is summoned to give as well as to receive, to be a "wellspring of the joy of living" as well as an "ocean depth of happy rest". Since this is so, it is reasonable to hold that within every human person, male or female, there is the "masculine" (the emphasis on giving in a receiving way, on being a "wellspring of the joy of living") and the "feminine" (the emphasis on receiving in a giving way, on being an "ocean depth of happy rest").[24] It is therefore possible to think of a man as a being who dynamically combines maleness, the masculine, and the feminine, while the woman is one who dynamically combines femaleness, the feminine, and the masculine. This in no way, however, as Prudence Allen among others has noted, implies that we are moving "to an androgyny, or a theory of identity of all human beings, because the starting point, the maleness or femaleness, is always different for the two sexes. The combination of the three factors of male, masculine, and feminine in a male individual would always differ from the combination of the three factors of female, masculine, and feminine in a female individual."[25] The point is that males and females, men and

[24] Joyce, *Human Sexual Ecology*, p. 68, expresses this idea by saying that his way of defining man and woman "takes into account that every person is male [I would say "masculine" rather than "male"] or female [I would say "feminine" rather than "female"] within. Every person has a human nature, which includes the ability and the tendency to share the gift of self. Both a man and a woman are structured in a way that naturally enables them to give in a receiving sort of way and to receive in a giving sort of way. . . . But the nature of man is a dynamic orientation to emphasize, at all levels of his being, the receiving kind of giving; while the nature of a woman is a dynamic orientation to emphasize, at all levels of her being, the giving kind of receiving."

[25] Sister Prudence Allen, "Integral Sexual Complementarity and the Theology of Communion", *Communio: International Catholic Review* 17 (1990): 533.

women, embrace within themselves the masculine and the feminine, but they embody and manifest these aspects of their personality in differing and complementary ways.

Precisely because the woman's sexuality emphasizes the withinness, the abidingness, the sameness of being and because the man's sexuality emphasizes the outgoingness, the expansiveness, the otherness of being, a woman's sexual identity is more interior, intimately linked to her being, her bodiliness, whereas a man's sexual identity is more exterior, intimately associated with his activity. It is for this reason, as numerous studies have shown,[26] that a woman more easily comes to a realization of what it means to be feminine and a woman than a man does in coming to realize what it means to be masculine and a man. The man needs, as it were, to go out of himself and prove himself in the world.

Insofar as they differ in their sexuality, men and women manifest major differences in their social behavior. Women, as many studies point out, tend toward responding to situations as entire persons, with their minds, bodies, and emotions integrated, whereas men tend to respond in a more diffuse and differentiated manner. Again, women are, on the whole, more oriented toward helping or caring for personal needs, whereas men, on the whole, are more inclined to formulate and pursue long-range goals and to achieve particular sets of prescribed

[26] See, for example, the following: J. Bardwick, *Psychology of Women* (New York: Harper & Row, 1971); Margaret Mead, *Male and Female* (New York: Dell, 1949); Robert Stoller, M.D., *Sex and Gender: On the Development of Masculinity and Femininity* (New York: Science House, 1968); Lionel Tiger, *Men in Groups* (New York: Random House, 1969). Their common point is that men need to go out of themselves in order to discover and secure their masculinity, whereas women do not. An interesting account of this issue is provided by Walter Ong, S.J., *Fighting for Life: Contest, Sexuality, and Consciousness* (Ithaca: Cornell University Press, 1981), esp. pp. 70–80, 97–98, 112–15. This accounts for the fact, as Ong notes, that "[T]he received symbol for woman, Venus' mirror (♀), adopted by feminists apparently everywhere, signifies self-possession, gazing at oneself as projected into the outside world or environment and reflected back into the self from there, whole. The received symbol for man, Mars' spear (♂), signifies conflict, change, stress, dissection, division" (p. 77).

ends.[27] Or, to put the matter somewhat differently, we might say, with Steven Clark, that "in social situations men are more oriented to goals outside the situation (what the situation can become), women to internal goals (relieving needs, giving comfort and pleasure)."[28] Note, however, that all this is a matter of *emphasis,* corresponding to the ways in which men and women tend to emphasize their sexuality. Men, too, can and do respond as entire persons and care for personal needs, and women, too, can and do differentiate between their emotions and their intelligent judgments and make long-range plans. But the tendencies noted are real and correspond to the personalities of men and women as sexual persons.

With this understanding of man and woman, male and female, and of their sexual complementarity in mind, we can now look more closely at the relationship between man and woman in marriage and to their vocation as fathers and mothers.

Woman as Mother, Man as Father

The marital act, which expresses and symbolizes the complementary sexuality of man and woman, is an act that is open not only to the communication of the unique and exclusive love proper to husbands and wives but also to the communication of life. For it is in and through the marital act that new human life comes to be in the way God wills that it come to be. New human life can, of course, come to be in and through the acts of adulterers and fornicators, and when it comes to be in this way, the new human life is indeed a new human person, a being to be loved and cherished and respected by all. But when new human life comes

[27] On this, see Steven Clark, *Man and Woman in Christ: An Examination of the Roles of Men and Women in Light of Scripture and the Social Sciences* (Ann Arbor, MI: Servant Books, 1980). In chapters sixteen and seventeen (pp. 371–466), Clark summarizes relevant material from the descriptive social sciences and experimental psychology bearing on the differences between males and females. Clark provides an exhaustive search of the literature, providing excellent bibliographical notes.

[28] Ibid., p. 390.

to be in this way, it is insulted and harmed, and a tragedy has occurred. For nonmarried men and women do not have the right to generate new human life, just as they do not have the right to engage in coition. They do not have the right to generate human life precisely because they have not, through their own free choice to marry one another, given to themselves the capacity to receive such life lovingly, to nourish it humanely, and to educate it in the love and service of God and neighbor.[29] This is an issue that has already been sufficiently considered above, in Chapter One.

God wills that new human life come to be in and through the loving marital act of husbands and wives. He does so because they have, precisely by virtue of the fact that they have given themselves unconditionally and unreservedly to one another in marriage, capacitated themselves to receive human life lovingly, nourish it humanely, and educate it in the love and service of God and neighbor. They are the ones who can give this new life the home that it needs to take root and grow.

When new human life comes to be in and through the marital act, it comes to be *within* the wife, within the mother. This new life, like every human life, is, as Pope John Paul II says, entrusted "to each and every other human being, but in a special way the human being is entrusted to woman, precisely because the woman in virtue of her special experience of motherhood is seen to have *a specific sensitivity* towards the human person and all that constitutes the individual's true welfare, beginning with the fundamental value of life."[30] Indeed, as the Holy Father also observes,

> Motherhood involves a special communion with the mystery of life as it develops in the woman's womb. The mother is filled with wonder at this mystery of life and "understands" with unique intuition what is happening inside her. In the light of

[29] St. Augustine, *De genesi ad literam,* 9, 7 (PL 34, 397).

[30] Pope John Paul II, *Christifideles laici,* no. 51. See also the Apostolic Letter *Mulieris dignitatem,* no. 30: "The moral and spiritual strength of a woman is joined to her awareness that *God entrusts the human being to her in a special way.* Of course, God entrusts every human being to each and every other human being. But this entrusting concerns women in a special way — precisely because of their femininity — and this in a particular way determines their vocation."

the "beginning", the mother accepts and loves as a person the child she is carrying in her womb. This unique contact with the new human being developing within her gives rise to an attitude toward human beings—not only towards her own child, but every human being—which profoundly marks the woman's personality. It is commonly thought that women are more capable than men of paying attention to another person and that motherhood develops this predisposition even more. The man—even with all his sharing in parenthood—always remains "outside" the process of pregnancy and the baby's birth; in many ways he has to *learn* his own *"fatherhood" from the mother*.... The mother's contribution is decisive in laying the foundation for a new human personality.[31]

We can see here how, in motherhood, the woman's sexuality as a "receiving in a giving sort of way" and as symbolizing the withinness of being and God as the "ocean depth of happy rest" is manifested. Moreover, as the Holy Father's remarks indicate, the tendency of women to respond integrally to situations, with mind, body, and emotions integrated, and to be oriented to personal needs is magnificently revealed in motherhood. In his comments, the Pope referred to the woman's "unique intuition" and "understanding" of what is going on within her. Here what he has to say fits in well with what we have seen before about the psychic-spiritual life of women and, indeed, seems to be corroborated by all that we know about their lives. I believe that Benedict Ashley has summarized this matter well. He writes:

From such empirical studies as are available, the common saying that women are more "intuitive" than men is probably correct. Human intelligence, as St. Thomas Aquinas pointed out, has two phases. The first phase is *intellectus, ratio superior,* "insight", or "intuition" by which we grasp certain seminal truths directly from our sense experience with a certainty based immediately on that experience. The second phase is *ratio, ratio inferior,* "reason", by which we explicitate and develop these seminal truths by a logical calculus.... It is not strange that women on the average rely more on insight, men on reason. While this can

[31] Pope John Paul II, *Mulieris dignitatem,* no. 18.

be attributed to the support given by our culture to these different modes of thought, yet they are perhaps more deeply and genetically rooted in the fact that women in order to succeed in their . . . role as mothers have needed a more penetrating intuition than do men in order to deal effectively with personal relations so needed in the family.[32]

The woman, therefore, is the one to whom new human life is entrusted in a very special way. But she is, precisely because of her sexuality and her way of imaging God, prepared to receive it lovingly and give it the care it needs in order to take root and grow.

It is important to stress here the immense contribution that mothers make to human civilization in carrying out responsibly their vocation to receive new human life and to care generously for it, especially during its early years.

But new human life is also entrusted to the man, to the husband. He is its father. But fathering, as indicated by Pope John Paul II in one of the passages cited above, is something that man must learn. Mothering, too, entails learning. But it is universally recognized that fatherhood and, in particular, the fatherhood necessary for a father-involved family, is much more a cultural achievement than is mothering.

In order for children, boys and girls, to develop well as integral persons, they need their fathers' care. Their fathers must become involved in their families.[33] The bond between children and their

---

[32] Benedict Ashley, O.P., "Moral Theology and Mariology", *Anthropotes: Rivista di studi sulla persona e la famiglia* 7, no. 2 (December 1991): 147. Ashley refers to Mary F. Belensky et al., *Women's Ways of Knowing: The Development of Self, Voice, and Mind* (New York: Basic Books, 1988), for an empirical study supporting the idea that women are more intuitive than men. He refers to St. Thomas, *Summa theologiae* 1, q. 79, a. 9, 2 *Sent.*, d. 24, q. 2, a. 2, and *De Veritate*, q. 15, a. 2, for the distinction between *intellectus, ratio superior* and *ratio, ratio inferior.*

[33] One of the greatest tragedies in contemporary American society is that 25 percent of all children under eighteen in the United States are raised by just one parent, usually a divorced or unmarried mother. More than sixteen million children in the United States currently live in single-parent households headed by a woman, deprived of their fathers' presence. On this, see *Beyond Rhetoric: A New American Agenda for Children and Families* (Final Report of the National Commission on

mother is strong by virtue of their symbiotic tie during pregnancy, birth, and nursing. Indeed, as John W. Miller has said, "it is this biologically determined relationship, so essential in laying the foundations of healthy development, that shapes those qualities usually associated with mothering: unconditional availability, receptivity, and tenderness."[34] But for the well-being of these children, the father's loving presence is needed. When they are effectively present to their families and to their children, fathers must, as Miller notes, "insert themselves into the bond between mother and child as a 'second other' by an initiative very much like that of adoption. Where this initiative is energetic and winsome", he continues:

> an essential autonomy from the mother is fostered and children of both sexes are significantly helped in orienting themselves to the cultural universe outside the home. . . . Maternal values are not thereby repudiated—fathers too may embody tender mother-like attributes without ceasing to be fathers—but the exclusivity of the mother-bond is challenged by an authority that separates the child and orients it toward its personal future in extra-familial society.[35]

But for fathers to succeed in this task, they must properly manifest their sexual complementarity to their wives and the mothers of their children. From all that has been said thus far, we can see that for fathers to do this they must be seen as those who emphatically give in a receiving sort of way, who image God as the wellspring of the joy of living. We have already seen that, on the whole, men tend to be more differentiated in their responses to persons and situations, to be more goal-oriented, and that their sexual identity depends to a much greater extent than does a

---

Children) (Washington, DC: National Commission on Children, 1991), pp. 4, 18.

The bad effects on children caused by the absence of their fathers are well described by Mary Stewart Van Leeuwen, *Gender and Grace: Love, Work, and Parenting in a Changing World* (Downers Grove, IL: InterVarsity Press, 1990), pp. 132–43, 182–83. See also David Blankenhorn, *Fatherless America* (New York: Basic Books, 1995).

[34] John W. Miller, *Biblical Faith and Fathering: Why We Call God "Father"* (New York: Paulist Press, 1989), p. 57.

[35] Ibid.

woman's on what they do. While a woman nurtures, a man, as Ashley puts it, "tends to *construct,* i.e., to impose an order on things, whether it is the simple physical fact of initiating pregnancy, providing the home as shelter and protection, or the more spiritual tasks of disciplining the children physically and mentally, or undertaking the work of the wider social order. Where the woman *allows* the child to grow, the father *causes* the child to grow."[36]

The father has the primary responsibility to provide his wife and his children with food, shelter, and protection, particularly during her pregnancy and their infancy, to give his children (and their mother) a sense of security by his presence and reliability. In saying that the father has the responsibility to provide for his wife and children, I do not mean to foreclose the possibility that in specific families the wife-mother may be the one who contributes more economically to the family. It may be that she has special talents and has acquired more marketably profitable capacities and could therefore more adequately meet the financial needs of the family than could the husband-father. But even in such situations, it is nonetheless still the husband-father's primary responsibility to see to it that the wife and children are provided for. Only if he is allowed to do so can he dynamically combine his maleness with the masculine and the feminine within him.

The father-involved family, as we have seen, is a fragile cultural achievement. And a family will be father-involved only if the husband-father is given the support necessary to be the one who gives in a receiving sort of way, who is the wellspring of the joy of living. If a culture ceases to support and encourage "through its mores, symbols, models, laws, and rituals, the sanctity of the bond between a man and his wife and a father's involvement with his own children, powerful natural forces will inevitably take over in favor of the mother-alone family."[37] And this is a tragedy.

Here it is important to realize that fathering and mothering are by no means mutually exclusive. The complementarity between males and females is sharply differentiated at their biological roots—only the woman can conceive and nurture the child within her

[36] Ashley, p. 140.
[37] Miller, p. 19.

womb and nurse it after birth. Nonetheless, the personality and
character traits (the "masculine" and the "feminine", the "wellspring
of the joy of living" and the "ocean depth of happy rest") are
present in both males and females, although, as we have seen, with
different emphases in each. Children need to be both accepted and
nurtured, to be challenged and held to standards, and both mothers
and fathers must accept and nurture their children, challenge them
and hold them to standards. But they do so in somewhat differing
modalities, with the mothers accentuating acceptance and nur-
turance, the fathers challenging and disciplining.[38]

Before concluding these reflections on marriage and male-
female complementarity, it is necessary to examine, albeit much
too briefly here, the significance of the third chapter of Genesis
and of the fifth chapter of Ephesians relative to marriage and the
complementarity of male and female.

Genesis 3:16 and Ephesians 5:21–33

The third chapter of Genesis tells the story of the disobedience of
man and woman (Adam and Eve) to God and their "fall". It shows
how their sin terribly harmed human persons and, in particular,
the male-female relationship in marriage. In punishing the woman
for her disobedience, God said: "Your desire shall be for your
husband, and he shall be your master" (Gen 3:16). As a result of
the fall, concupiscence entered the human heart. Because of their
physical strength and because the biology of the generative process
allows men more opportunities to abuse their role, husbands and
fathers, unfortunately, have often led the way in irresponsibility.
Mothers and wives have, on the other hand, been tempted to

---

[38] Worthwhile observations concerning the indispensable help fathers can give
their children by communicating to them the knowledge and techniques they need
to deal with the wider world by setting standards and challenging them are
provided by Basil Cole, O.P., "Reflexions pour une spiritualité masculine", trans.
Guy Bedouelle, O.P., *Sources* (Fribourg) 12 (March–April 1987): 49–55. See also
James B. Stenson, *Successful Fathers,* Scepter Booklet No. 181/182 (Princeton, N.J.:
Scepter, 1989) and Blankenhorn, pp. 201–54.

become manipulative.[39] A "re-creation" of human persons, male and female, and of marriage itself was needed.

This "re-creation", thanks to God's bounteous mercy and goodness, has indeed taken place. For he has sent us his Son to redeem us and to bring us to a new kind of life. Through the saving death and Resurrection of Jesus, we have been liberated from sin and made new creatures. Through baptism we die to the "old man", to Adamic man, to sinful man, and put on the new man, Christ.

The marriage of Christians, of those who have, through baptism, become one with Christ and members of his body, is moreover a sacrament. It is a holy sign of the life-giving, love-giving union between Christ and his Bride, the Church. And not only is it a holy sign of this life-giving, love-giving union, but it is also, for those men and women who clothe themselves with Christ and abide in his love, an *effective* sign of this union, one that they can, with God's grace, realize in their own married lives, and in this way they mediate to the world the redemptive love of Christ. As Pope John Paul II has said,

> The Spirit which the Lord pours forth gives a new heart, and renders man and woman capable of loving one another as Christ has loved us. Conjugal love reaches that fullness to which it is interiorly ordained, conjugal charity, which is the proper and specific way in which the spouses participate in and are called to live the very charity of Christ, who gave himself on the cross.[40]

Indeed, as Pope John Paul II continues, "by means of baptism, man and woman are definitively placed within the new and eternal covenant, in the spousal covenant of Christ with the Church. And it is because of this indestructible insertion that the intimate community of conjugal life and love, founded by the Creator, is elevated and assumed into the spousal charity of Christ, sustained and enriched by his redeeming power." Because of this, "spouses are . . . the permanent reminder to the Church of what

---

[39] On this, see the perceptive comments of Van Leeuwen, pp. 44–48.

[40] Pope John Paul II, *Familiaris consortio*, no. 13.

happened on the cross; they are for one another and for their children witnesses to the salvation in which the sacrament makes them sharers."[41]

The beauty of Christian marriage as an image of the bridal relationship between Christ and his Church is set forth eloquently in the Epistle to the Ephesians, where we read:

> Defer to one another out of reverence for Christ. Wives should be submissive to their husbands, as if to the Lord, because the husband is the head of his wife just as Christ is head of his body the church, as well as its savior. As the church submits to Christ, so wives should submit to their husbands in everything.
>
> Husbands, love your wives, as Christ loved the church. He gave himself up for her to make her holy, purifying her in the bath of water by the power of the word, to present to himself a glorious church, holy and immaculate, without stain or wrinkle or anything of that sort. Husbands should love their wives as they do their own bodies. He who loves his wife loves himself. Observe that no one ever hates his own flesh; no, he nourishes it and takes care of it as Christ cares for the church—for we are members of his body.
>
> "For this reason a man shall leave his father and mother, and shall cling to his wife, and the two shall be made into one." This is a great mystery. I mean that it refers to Christ and the church. In any case, each one should love his own wife as he loves himself, the wife for her part showing respect for the husband (Eph 5:21–33).

Here I cannot attempt to comment at length on this passage.[42] Today this text is, unfortunately, not held in honor by some, who believe that it is demeaning to women insofar as it speaks of the wife's "submission" to her husband, who is characterized as her "head". My remarks here will be limited to the issues of submission and headship.

---

[41] Ibid.

[42] A very perceptive and thoughtful commentary on this text is provided by Hans Urs Von Balthasar, "Ephesians 5:21–33 and *Humanae Vitae:* A Meditation", in *Christian Married Love,* ed. Raymond Dennehy (San Francisco: Ignatius Press, 1981), pp. 55–73.

Pope John Paul II has, I believe, done much to help us understand this passage in its total context within the good news of salvation and in this way to appreciate properly the "submission" involved in marriage. In his commentary on this passage, he first observes that the exhortation to husbands to love their wives as Christ loved the Church summons not only husbands but all men to be imitators of Christ in their dealings with women. And in Christ's love "there is a fundamental affirmation of the woman as person." Continuing, he then says:

> The author of the Letter to the Ephesians sees no contradiction between an exhortation formulated in this way and the words: "Wives, be subject to your husbands, as to the Lord. For the husband is the head of the wife" (Eph 5:22-23). The author knows that this way of speaking, so profoundly rooted in the customs and religious tradition of the time, is to be understood and carried out in a new way; as a *"mutual subjection out of reverence for Christ"* (cf. Eph 5:21). This is especially true because the husband is called the "head" of the wife *as* Christ is the head of the Church; he is so in order to give "himself up for her" (Eph 5:25), and giving himself up for her means giving up even his own life. However, whereas in the relationship between Christ and the Church the subjection is only on the part of the Church, in the relationship between husband and wife the "subjection" is not one-sided but mutual.[43]

From this it is clear that this passage in no way countenances male domination, nor does it impose on wives a one-sided subjection to their husbands. The intention of the sacred writer is to call Christian husbands and wives to live their marriage relationship in mutual self-sacrifice, after the model of Christ.

With respect to the "headship" of the husband and of the father in the family, I hold that there is a genuine truth, necessary for the father-involved family, at stake. I will briefly attempt to show why.

First of all, there is need for authority in any human community. Authority, however, must not be confused with domination and

---

[43] Pope John Paul II, *Mulieris dignitatem*, no. 24.

the exercise of power; indeed, domination and the exercise of power are abuses of authority. Authority is, rather, a necessary principle of cooperation and thus a role of service to the community. Marriage and family life involve cooperative action and require unified decisions, and to make decisions is the proper task of authority within marriage and the family, as it is within any human community.

Authority, in short, is not domination but decision making. Husbands and wives surely share in this authority, which usually entails common deliberation and often results in consensus. But at times decision-making authority cannot be exercised in this way. Emergencies arise, when there is little or no possibility for common deliberation and consent. At other times, consensus may not emerge. Yet, for the common good of the marriage and of the spouses, authority must be exercised by one spouse or the other. It seems to me that here the complementary differences between male and female are relevant and that these differences support the view that the husband is the one who is required to exercise this authority.

This is commonly the case in emergency conditions. The identity of the one who is to exercise authority must be clear when emergencies arise, and several attributes of the husband are crucial in such emergencies: his size and strength, his capacity for setting long-range goals and particular objectives for reaching them, his capacity for differentiating. When emergencies arise that require the cooperation of both spouses (and, at times, the children as well), the husband-father is often the one best suited to make and execute decisions. If authority in family emergencies pertains to the husband-father, it is fitting that he exercise it for the family as a whole in other instances when this is required — when cooperation is essential but no consensus can be reached. The proper exercise of this authority is by no means a matter of domination but rather a gift to the marriage and to the family. In order for the husband to exercise his authority properly, he must be willing to be self-sacrificial and to subordinate his own individual interests to the well-being and good of the marriage and the family.[44] In this way he will manifest his love for his wife and reveal and relive on earth "the very fatherhood of God", ensuring "the harmonious and united development of all the members of the family".[45]

Conclusion

Marriage is the "creation of a lasting personal union between a man and a woman based on love".[46] It is a communion of persons intended to bear witness on earth and to image the intimate communion of persons within the Trinity.[47] It is a sacrament of the love-giving, life-giving bridal union between Christ and his Church, ordered to the procreation and education of children who are to be lovingly received, nurtured humanely, and educated in the love and service of God.

This beautiful partnership, this wonderful covenant of love, unites human persons who differ in their sexuality and complement each other. Both husband and wife are to give and to receive; both are to image God as the "wellspring of the joy of living" and the "ocean depth of happy rest". But each is to do so in his and her indispensably complementary ways, the husband emphatically giving in a receiving sort of way and serving as the "wellspring of the joy of living", and the wife emphatically receiving in a giving sort of way and serving as the "ocean depth of happy rest". Their marital love, exclusive of others in the intimacy of their partnership of life and their one-flesh union, is the kind of love that is inclusive insofar as it reaches out to others

[44] The considerations given here regarding the authority of the husband-father are developed more fully by Germain Grisez in *Living a Christian Life*, vol. 2 of his *The Way of the Lord Jesus* (Quincy, IL: Franciscan College Press, 1993), pp. 629–33.

[45] Pope John Paul II, *Familiaris consortio*, no. 25.

[46] Karol Wojtyla, p. 218.

[47] On this matter, the excellent essay of Mary Rousseau is most helpful. See her "Pope John Paul II's *Letter on the Dignity and Vocation of Women:* The Call to *Communio*", *Communio: International Catholic Review* 16 (1989): 212–32.

and bears fruit in the world in which they live, as they joyously accept the gift of children and serve the needs of the society in which they live. The home based on the union of man and woman in Christian marriage is indeed a "domestic Church".[48] a witness to the truth that God is a loving Father and that the Church is our mother, and that all human persons, male and female, are called to love and communion.

[48] See Vatican Council II, Dogmatic Constitution *Lumen gentium*, no. 11; *Apostolicam actuositatem* [Decree on the Lay Apostolate], no. 11; Pope John Paul II, *Familiaris consortio*, no. 49. See also *Catechism of the Catholic Church*, nos. 1655–58, pp. 413–14; nos. 2204–6, p. 532. See below, Chapter Five.

3

Pope Paul VI: A True Prophet

The proper biblical and theological understanding of a prophet is that of a person who is an accredited witness of God's revelation, who can expound it rightly in the concrete situation facing him and his environment. Precisely because his appraisal of the issues confronting him and the people in the light of God's revelation requires him to consider the future, the prophet can interpret the present in view of its dynamism for the future—"prophecy" in the ordinary sense of the term today.[1]

Given this understanding of a prophet, I believe it is quite correct to regard Pope Paul VI as a true prophet and his Encyclical *Humanae vitae* as a prophetic document. This is precisely the view of Pope John Paul II and others.[2] Paul VI is a prophet because he

[1] On this, see Karl Rahner and Herbert Vorgrimler, *Dictionary of Theology*, 2d ed. (New York: Crossroad, 1985), p. 419.

[2] See Pope John Paul II, Apostolic Exhortation *Familiaris consortio*, no. 29, where he says: "Precisely because the love of husband and wife is a unique participation in the mystery of life and of the love of God Himself, the Church knows that she has received the special mission of guarding and protecting the lofty dignity of marriage and the most serious responsibility of the transmission of human life. Thus, in continuity with the living tradition of the ecclesiastical community throughout history, the recent Second Vatican Council and the Magisterium of my predecessor Paul VI, expressed above all in the Encyclical *Humanae vitae*, have handed on to our times a truly prophetic proclamation, which reaffirms and reproposes with clarity the Church's teaching and norm, always old yet always new, regarding marriage and regarding the transmission of human life."

On the prophetic character of *Humanae vitae*, see the excellent book of Dionigi

both clearly affirms central truths of human existence in the light of divine revelation, accurately assesses some of the major issues facing men and women of our day, and foresees the terrible harms that human persons will suffer by abandoning God's design for marriage and the family.

To show the prophetic character of *Humanae vitae,* I believe that it will be helpful, first of all (1), to consider the "integral vision" of human persons set forth in this Encyclical, according to which there is an intimate and unbreakable bond uniting sex, love, and procreation, and, secondly (2), to examine the "disintegrative vision" of human persons underlying the acceptance of contraception, a vision dissolving this bond and, as a result, bringing to human persons the harms that Pope Paul feared would come about should God's plan for human existence be put aside. In conclusion, I will try to show the truth of Pope John Paul II's belief that the differences between these two "visions" is ultimately rooted in "two irreconcilable concepts of the human person and of human sexuality".[3]

1. The "Integral Vision" of Human Persons and the Bond Uniting Sex, Love, and Procreation.

Paul VI wisely observed that the specific question taken up in *Humanae vitae,* namely, the most important mission [*munus*][4] of married men and women to hand on life to new human persons, can be addressed adequately only within the context provided by

---

Tettamanzi, *Un'enciclica profetica: La Humanae vitae vent'anni dopo* (Milan: Editrice Ancora Milano, 1988).

[3] John Paul II, *Familiaris consortio,* no. 32.

[4] On the rich meaning of the Latin term *munus,* used by Pope Paul VI to designate the "mission" of married couples to hand on life to new human persons, see Janet Smith, "The *Munus* of Transmitting Human Life: A New Approach to *Humanae Vitae*", *Thomist* 54 (July 1990): 385–427. See also her *Humanae Vitae: A Generation Later* (Washington, DC: The Catholic University of America Press, 1991), pp. 136–48.

an "integral vision" of the human person, a vision illumined by divine revelation.[5] In particular, he reminded us that this question must be examined in the light of God's plan for marriage and for human existence: "God the Creator wisely and providently established marriage with the intent that He might achieve His own design of love through Men. Therefore, through mutual self-giving, which is unique [*proprium*] and exclusive to them, spouses seek a communion of persons [*personarum communionem*]. Through this communion, the spouses perfect each other so that they might share with God the task [*operam socient*] of procreating and educating new living beings."[6]

In this passage, Pope Paul speaks of the "mutual self-giving . . . unique and exclusive" to spouses. Marriage comes to be only when a man and a woman, by an act of irrevocable personal consent, give themselves to one another unreservedly and unconditionally. Their marital union is consummated and expressed in the act which is unique and exclusive to them, the marital act. Later in the Encyclical, speaking of the marital act, Paul has this to say: "Because of its intrinsic nature [*intimam rationem*] the conjugal act, while uniting husband and wife in the most intimate of bonds, also *makes them fit* [*eos idoneos facit*] to bring forth new life according to the laws written into their very nature as male and female."[7] Note that he says that the conjugal act "*makes them* [*spouses*] *fit to* bring forth new life *according to the laws written into their very nature as male and female*". As I now hope to show, this is a sublime truth which greatly helps us to see the wisdom of "God's plan" for human existence.

Although human life, no matter how it comes to be, must be recognized and respected as sacred from the first moment of

[5] Paul VI, Encyclical *Humanae vitae*, no. 7; in this essay, except where noted, I will use the translation of *Humanae vitae* from the Latin text as provided by Janet Smith in her *Humanae Vitae: A Generation Later*. Number 7 is found on pp. 276–77 of her book.

[6] Ibid., no. 8; Smith trans., pp. 277–78.

[7] Ibid., no. 12. Here I have modified slightly Smith's translation to bring out more clearly the force of the Latin "*eos ideneos facit*".

conception,[8] God does not will that new human life come to be through the random copulation of unmarried males and females. As we saw in Chapter One, unmarried men and women have no right to generate human life through their acts of fornication, simply because they have not, through their own free choice, capacitated themselves to receive such life lovingly, nourish it humanely, and educate it in the love and service of God; they have not capacitated themselves to cooperate with God in raising up new human persons "according to the laws written into their very nature as males and females".[9]

Nor do unmarried males and females have a "right" to copulate. They do not have this right because they have refused, by their own free choice, to capacitate themselves to respect each other as irreplaceable and nonsubstitutable persons in their freely chosen acts of fornication.

But husbands and wives have the right to the marital act. By giving themselves to one another in marriage, husbands and wives have capacitated themselves to give one another conjugal love and to receive human life lovingly from God, to nourish it humanely, and to educate it in his love and service.

The marital act as a moral and human act, moreover, is not simply a genital act between a man and woman who *happen* to be married. It is an act that inwardly participates in their one-flesh, marital union and in the "goods" or "blessings" of marriage, that is, the goods of loving fidelity and of children. The *marital* act, therefore, as distinct from a mere *genital* act, is one that is (1) open to the communication of spousal love and (2) open to God's gift of new human life, the "supreme gift of marriage".[10]

---

[8] On this, see John XXIII, Encyclical *Mater et magistra*, AAS 53 (1961): 447; cited explicitly by Paul VI in *Humanae vitae*, no. 13, n. 13. See also Vatican Council II, Pastoral Constitution *Gaudium et spes*, no. 51.

[9] St. Augustine, *De genesi ad literam*, 9, 7; PL 34, 397. St. Augustine insisted that children are a *good*, a *blessing* of marriage, which God established precisely so that "the chastity of women would make children known to their fathers and fathers to their children. True, it was possible for men to be born of promiscuous and random intercourse with any women at all, but there could not have been a bond of kinship between fathers and children." *Contra Julianum*, 5, 9; PL 44, 806.

[10] Vatican Council II, *Gaudium et spes*, no. 49.

Paul himself indicates the difference between a marital act as a moral and human act and a "marital" act understood purely descriptively as a genital act between a man and a woman who "happen" to be married. In a singularly perceptive passage he writes: "People rightly understand that a conjugal act [that is, a "marital" act in the purely descriptive sense] imposed on a spouse, with no consideration given to the condition of the spouse or to the legitimate desires of the spouse, is not a true act of love. They understand that such an act opposes what the moral order rightly requires from spouses", that is, they understand that such an act does not truly participate in the marriage itself and in the "goods" of marriage. Quite to the contrary, it violates the good of marital unity and friendship.[11] He goes on to say: "To be consistent, then, if they reflect further, they should acknowledge that it is necessarily true that an act of mutual love that impairs the capacity of bringing forth life contradicts both the divine plan that established the nature [normam] of the conjugal bond and also the will of the first Author of human life. For this capacity of bringing forth life was designed by God, the Creator of All, according to [his] specific laws."[12] An act of this kind, although "marital" in a purely descriptive sense, does not, any more than an act of spousal abuse, participate inwardly in the marriage and in the "goods" of marriage. To the contrary, an act of this kind violates the marital good of procreation because the spouses have, through their own free choice, shut it off, "closed" it, to God's gift of children.

Precisely because the marital act, as a human and moral act, is open both to the expression of spousal love and to the reception of God's gift of life to new human persons, there is inherent in it, as Pope Paul affirmed, "an unbreakable bond, established by God, which man is not permitted to break on his own initiative, between its unitive meaning and its procreative meaning."[13] There is, in

[11] Paul VI, *Humanae vitae,* no. 13; Smith trans., pp. 281–82.

[12] Ibid., no. 13; Smith trans., p. 282.

[13] Ibid., no. 12. Here I have not followed the Smith translation. See also Pius XII, "Address to Participants in the Second Naples World Congress on Fertility and Human Sterility", May 19, 1956; AAS 48 (1956): 470.

short, a bond uniting sex, love, and the procreation of new human life. And what God has joined together, let no man put asunder.

Moreover, because every human person is a being made in God's image and likeness and is called to a life in union with God in Christ, *no human person ought ever to be unwanted, that is, unloved.* And to secure a society in which all human persons, including children, are indeed wanted and loved, it is absolutely imperative that men and women respect the bond uniting sex, love, and the transmission of human life, that they honor marriage and the marriage bed (cf. Heb 13:4), and open their hearts and homes to God's gift of children by letting the little children come to him (cf. Lk 18:15–16).

Thus contraception is an intrinsically immoral act precisely because it severs the bond uniting sex, love, and the procreation of human life. It is, indeed, an *anti-life* kind of act, through which men and women deliberately "close" their freely chosen acts of intimate union to God's gift of life.[14] The anti-life nature of contraception is evident from a consideration of what contraception is. Pope Paul accurately describes the nature of contraception by identifying it as "every action, which, either in anticipation of the conjugal act [or indeed of any genital act], or in its accomplishment, or in the development of its natural consequences, proposes [*intendat*], either as end or as means, to impede procreation [*ut procreatio impediatur*]."[15] In other words, what one does when one

---

[14] On this, see Germain Grisez, Joseph Boyle, John Finnis, and William E. May, " 'Every Marital Act Ought to Be Open to New Life': Toward a Clearer Understanding", *Thomist* 52 (1988): 367–426.

In her helpful study, *Humanae Vitae: A Generation Later,* Janet Smith considers this argument "inadequate" and a departure from the Catholic tradition. For a friendly and appreciative critique of her work, in which I show how she has, unfortunately, misunderstood our argument and has also failed to take into account the traditional Catholic understanding of contraception as an anti-life act, see my review of her book in the *Thomist* 57 (1993): 155–61. On the traditional understanding of contraception as anti-life, see the following note.

[15] Paul VI, *Humanae vitae,* no. 14. Here I have not used Janet Smith's translation because she translates the Latin word *intendat* as "chooses". Paul VI, however, was definitely using this Latin term in the senses in which it was used by St. Thomas, as designating *both* the intending of the end (*voluntas intendens*) *and* the choosing of

contracepts is to impede the beginning of a new human life. A person contracepts only because he or she, wishing to engage in

---

means (*voluntas eligens*), as the text of Paul VI makes clear, since he speaks of "intending" or "proposing" to impede procreation either as one's *end* or means.

Pope Paul himself stressed the anti-life character of contraception in a homily given ten years after the publication of *Humanae vitae*: "Homily on the Feast of Sts. Peter and Paul", June 29, 1978, AAS 70 (1978): 397; printed in *L'Osservatore Romano*, English ed., July 6, 1978, p. 3. Here he refers to *Humanae vitae* as a defense of life "at the very source of human existence", a document which "drew its inspiration from the inviolable teaching of the Bible and the Gospel, which confirms the norms of the natural law and the unsuppressible dictates of conscience on respect for life, the transmission of which is entrusted to responsible fatherhood and motherhood." Moreover, in footnote 14 of *Humanae vitae,* he explicitly referred to the teaching of the *Roman Catechism* (popularly known as *The Catechism of the Council of Trent*), which was universally used in the Church from the end of the sixteenth century until the middle of this century, in which contraception, like abortion, is branded an anti-life, homicidal kind of act. The *Roman Catechism* affirmed that "whoever, joined in marriage, either impede conception by medicines or expel the child conceived, commit a most grave crime, for this must be considered the impious conspiracy of homicides" (pt. 2, chap. 8, no. 13: the Latin text reads: "Fit ut illorum sit scelus gravissimum qui, Matrimonio iuncti, medicamentis vel conceptum impediunt, vel partum abigunt, haec enim homicidarum impia conspiratio existimanda est"). The teaching of this Catechism, in turn, is rooted in the centuries-old canon, the *Si aliquis,* which formed part of the Church's universal law from the thirteenth century until 1917: "If anyone for the sake of fulfilling sexual desire or with premeditated hatred does something to a man or to a woman, or gives something to drink, so that he cannot generate, or she cannot conceive, or offspring be born, let it be held as homicide" (Latin text: "Si aliquis causa explendae libidinis vel odii meditatione homini aut mulieri aliquid fecerit, vel ad potandum dederit, ut non possit generare, aut concipere, vel nasci soboles, ut homicida teneatur"). Text in *Decret. Greg. IX,* lib. V, titl. 12, cap. v; *Corpus iuris canonici,* ed. A. L. Richter and A. Friedberg (Leipzig: Tauchnitz, 1881), 2:794.

John Paul II has often noted the anti-life nature of contraception. See, for example, his "Homily at Mass for Youth", Nairobi, Kenya, August 17, 1985; *Insegnamenti di Giovanni Paolo II,* 8:2 (Rome: Libreria Editrice Vaticana, 1985), p. 453; printed in *L'Osservatore Romano,* English ed., August 26, 1985, p. 5. In this homily, after pointing out that the fullest sign of self-giving is when couples willingly accept children and quoting *Gaudium et spes,* no. 50, John Paul II says: "That is why anti-life actions such as contraception and abortion are wrong and are unworthy of good husbands and wives."

The anti-life character of contraception is also clearly noted in the *Catechism of the Catholic Church,* which affirms that "the Church, which 'is on the side of life'

genital sex—an act reasonably held to be the kind of act through which a new human life can come to be—does not want that new human life to come to be. Therefore, he or she does something prior to this freely chosen genital act, during it, or after it, precisely to impede or prevent that new human life from beginning. Should a new human life begin despite one's contraceptive efforts to impede its beginning, it comes to be as an "unwanted child", as St. Augustine noted in his *Confessions,* when, despite the contraceptive acts which he and his mistress engaged in, a child was conceived and born "against their wills".[16]

Moreover, when contraception is practiced by married couples, it is not only an anti-life kind of act, but an anti-love kind of act. By dissolving the bond uniting the unitive and procreative meanings of the conjugal act, contraception, as John Paul II and others have pointed out, "alters the value of 'total' self-giving". Through contraception, "the innate language that expresses the total reciprocal self-giving of husband and wife is overlaid . . . by an objectively contradictory language, namely, that of not giving oneself totally to the other. This leads not only to a positive refusal to be open to life but also to a falsification of the inner truth of conjugal love, which is called upon to give itself in personal totality."[17] Indeed, they change the moral character of the act of genital union. It is no longer a "marital act" in the human, moral sense, for it no longer participates inwardly in the marriage and in the goods or blessings of marriage. It is deliberately closed both to the full-giving characteristic of marital love and to God's gift of life.

It is important to understand that the two meanings of the

[*Familiaris consortio,* no. 30], teaches that 'each and every marriage act must remain open to the transmission of life' [*Humanae vitae,* no. 11]" (no. 2366).

[16] St. Augustine, *Confessions,* bk. 4, chap. 2.

[17] John Paul II, *Familiaris consortio,* no. 32. The *Catechism of the Catholic Church* makes this teaching of Pope John Paul II its own; see no. 2370, p. 570. John Paul II, who foreshadowed this line of argumentation in his *Love and Responsibility,* written originally in 1960 and translated into English in 1981 (New York: Farrar, Straus, and Giroux, 1981; reprinted, San Francisco: Ignatius Press, 1993), has developed it beautifully in his Wednesday audiences devoted to the development of a "theology of the body". His thought on this issue is presented accurately and attractively by Smith in *Humanae Vitae: A Generation Later,* pp. 107–18, 230–65.

marital act, the unitive and the procreative, do not lie side-by-side, as it were, stuck together, but are even closer than that: the life-giving aspect of the marital act is part of its love-giving meaning. The two are inseparable because *no whole can be without its essential parts.* [18] The *Catechism of the Catholic Church* expresses this profound truth by saying: "A child does not come from outside as something added on to the mutual love of the spouses, but springs from the very heart of that mutual giving, as its fruit and fulfillment."[19]

Thus, central to the "integral vision" of human existence, rooted in divine revelation, at the heart of Pope Paul's prophetic Encyclical is the truth that there is an inherent bond uniting sex, love, and procreation. The goods, the blessings, of human sexuality are love and life; the union of husbands and wives, like the union of Christ with his Church, is a life-giving, love-giving union that welcomes new human life as a precious gift from God.

2. The "Disintegrative Vision" of Human Persons and the Dissolving of the Bond Uniting Sex, Love, and Procreation

Yet this truth, unfortunately, has been cast aside today by many, and in its place we find a vision of human sexuality and of human persons that has torn asunder the intrinsic bond uniting sex, love, and the handing on of human life. This understanding — or, more accurately — this terrible *mis*understanding of human sexuality and of human persons — is exactly the misunderstanding of

[18] On this, see Germain Grisez, *The Way of the Lord Jesus*, vol. 2, *Living a Christian Life* (Quincy, IL: Franciscan College Press, 1993): 633–36. See also Francis X. Meehan, "Contemporary Theological Developments on Sexuality", in *Human Sexuality and Personhood* (St. Louis: Pope John XXIII Center, 1981), p. 177: "Sexuality implies by its very bodily phenomenon a human-life dimension. What is often not understood, and what I would like to emphasize here, is that life and love are really not two separate meanings but are inherently connected and mutually conditioned. For this reason *Humanae vitae* is more than a teaching on birth control: it is an anthropological insight suggesting that love calls for life — indeed so much so that any lack of orientation toward life actually flaws the love."

[19] *Catechism of the Catholic Church*, no. 2366, p. 569.

human sexuality undergirding the widespread acceptance of contraception.

The noted biologist Ashley Montagu well expressed the new, contraceptive vision of human sexuality in an essay, written about the same time as *Humanae vitae,* in which he celebrated the discovery of the "pill", likening it to the discovery of fire and the invention of the wheel. According to Montagu, "the pill makes it possible to render every individual of reproductive age completely responsible for both his sexual and his reproductive behavior. *It is necessary*", he wrote, "*to be unequivocally clear concerning the distinction between sexual behavior and reproductive behavior.* Sexual behavior may have no purpose other than pleasure ... without the slightest intent of reproducing, or it may be indulged in for both pleasure and reproduction."[20] Or to put it another way, "making love" is one thing, "making babies" is another.

On this view there is no longer any need, as there was in the whole past history of the race, to be overly concerned about "reproducing" in an act of genital sex. Thanks to the pill and other developments in contraceptive technology, mankind has been liberated from this fear. Indeed, the taboos imposed on sexual behavior in the past because of its association with reproduction no longer need to inhibit human choices. On this view it is obvious that the most frequent and durably most important meaning of sexual union consists in its ability to help human persons fulfill their need for orgasmic pleasure and to communicate affection.[21]

This mentality gives rise to the slogan, very popular and unquestionably accepted by most people in our culture, that "no unwanted child ought ever to be born." To prevent the tragedy of the birth of an "unwanted child" it is obviously imperative to have recourse to contraception and, should contraception fail, to abortion. But, on the other hand, persons who ardently desire a child ought to be able to have one, even if this means "producing" the child in the laboratory by *in vitro* fertilization and other techniques of

---

[20] Ashley Montagu, *Sex, Man, and Society* (New York: G. P. Putnam's, 1969), pp. 13–14. Emphasis in the original.

[21] On this, see the perceptive comments of George Gilder, *Sexual Suicide* (New York: Quadrangle Books, 1973), p. 34.

"artful babymaking".[22] On this view, children become objects of human desire, "wanted" if desired, "unwanted" if not desired. Their generation is transformed from an act of procreation to one of reproduction. They are treated, not as persons equal in dignity to their parents, but as products subordinated to the desires of their producers and subject to quality controls and cast aside if discovered to be "defective".

This contraceptive, disintegrative vision of human sexuality locates the human and personal value of sex in its relational purposes, in its ability to help people escape from the prison of loneliness and to enter into meaningful relationships with significant others and, in so doing, to enjoy themselves and find refreshment and ecstasy.[23] The procreative character of human sexuality,

---

[22] Joseph Fletcher expresses this view quite lucidly. He writes: "Man is a maker and a selector and a designer, and the more rationally contrived and deliberate anything is, the more human it is. Any attempt to set up an antimony between natural and biological reproduction, on the one hand, and artificial and designed reproduction, on the other, is absurd. The real difference is between accidental or random reproduction and rationally willed or chosen reproduction.... It [the latter] is willed, chosen, purposed, and controlled, and surely these are among the traits that distinguish *homo sapiens* from others in the animal genus, from the primates down. Genital reproduction is, therefore, less human than laboratory reproduction, more fun, to be sure, *but with our separation of baby-making from love-making* both become more human because they are matters of choice, not chance." In "Ethical Aspects of Genetic Controls", *New England Journal of Medicine* 285 (1971): 781–82. Emphasis added.

[23] This is clearly the way human sexuality is understood in contemporary American culture and by such influential writers as Montagu and Alex Comfort (author of *The Joy of Sex*). On this see, for example, Perry London's article "Sexual Behavior" in the standard reference work *Encyclopedia of Bioethics*, ed. Warren T. Reich (New York: Macmillan-Free Press, 1978), 4:1560–69. It is also the way human sexuality is understood by those Catholic theologians who reject the teaching of *Humanae vitae* and hold that contraception can be a morally good, indeed, necessary choice. On this see, for instance, Louis Janssens, the noted Belgian theologian who for many years was professor of moral theology at Louvain University. According to Janssens, "the most profound meaning of human sexuality is that it is a relational reality, having a special significance for the person in his relationships." "Considerations on *Humanae Vitae*", *Louvain Studies* 2 (1969): 249. See also Anthony Kosnik et al., *Human Sexuality: New Directions in American Catholic Thought*. A Study Commissioned by the Catholic Theological Society of America (New York: Paulist Press, 1977).

or, as advocates of contraception prefer to say, the "reproductive" aspect of human sexuality, is considered to be, of itself, subpersonal and subhuman, becoming personal and human only when "assumed into the human sphere", that is, by being consciously willed and chosen.[24]

It logically follows, when the human significance of sex is seen in this way, that the principal criterion for evaluating sexual activity focuses on the quality of the relationship established or expressed by such activity. Thus, while hardly anyone in our contraceptive culture commends callous, cruel, or exploitative sexual activity, the opinion is pervasive that any kind of genital activity is permissible so long as it is "responsible". By this is meant genital activity that is caring and sensitive to the needs of the partner and that safeguards against sexually transmitted diseases, such as herpes and AIDS, and unwanted pregnancies.

There is no need, on this view, for sexual partners to be married, although this may be considered the ideal. In fact, there is no need that they be of opposite sex, for, after all, homosexually oriented persons, male and female, have the same desire to communicate affection and relieve sexual tensions through orgasm as do heterosexually oriented individuals. Indeed, there is today the demand that the "holy unions" of committed homosexuals be granted the same status as heterosexual marriages.[25]

Some advocates of contraception, principally dissenting Catholic theologians, want to retain, at least to some extent, the bond

[24] On this, see one of the "Majority Reports" of the Papal Commission on Population, the Family, and Natality, *Documentum syntheticum de paternitate responsabili,* translated as "The Question Is Not Closed", in *The Birth Control Debate,* ed. Robert Hoyt (Kansas City: National Catholic Reporter, 1968), p. 71.

[25] See, for instance, Brent Hartinger, "A Case for Gay Marriage", in *Perspectives on Marriage: A Reader,* ed. Kieran Scott and Michael Warren (New York: Oxford University Press, 1993), pp. 130–35. It is noteworthy that this essay, and others of a similar calibre, appears in an anthology specifically designed by the editors as a text for use in courses on the theology of marriage taught in Roman Catholic colleges and universities. No article in the work supports the teaching of *Humanae vitae,* and several explicitly endorse contraception, divorce and remarriage, and homosexual unions.

uniting sex, marital love, and the generation of human life by linking procreation to the whole of marriage and not to freely chosen marital acts.[26] But the logic underlying the acceptance of contraception, which holds that men indeed have the right to sever the bond uniting sex, love, and procreation, is grounded in the disintegrative vision of human sexuality and of human persons so well expressed by Montagu and others. This has been frankly acknowledged by the more consistent and plain-speaking dissenting theologians.[27]

What all this shows us is that, as Paul VI clearly foresaw in his prophetic Encyclical, once the reasons alleged to justify contraception are accepted, there would follow a "gradual weakening in the discipline of morals". Surely prophetic was his admonition that "not much experience is needed to understand human weakness and to comprehend that human beings, especially the young, are so susceptible to temptation that they need to be encouraged to keep the moral law. It is wrong to make it easy for them to violate

---

[26] Thus many theologians accept the argument justifying contraception on the basis of the "totality" of marriage and marital acts. This argument, which is quite specious, was first presented in one of the "Majority Reports" of the Papal Commission on Population, the Family, and Natality. In the *Documentum syntheticum de paternitate responsabili* ("The Question Is Not Closed"), the authors of this report claim, fallaciously, that individual contracepted marital acts are *not* specified by the intent to impede the beginning of new human life but rather by the totality of marriage and that what contracepting married persons were actually doing was simply "fostering love responsibly toward a generous fecundity". To describe contraception in this way is really to conceal its nature and to *redescribe* it in terms of its hoped-for results or consequences. See "The Question Is Not Closed" in *The Birth Control Debate*, p. 72. For a critique of this fallacious argument, see, for instance, my *Absolutes in Moral Theology: Catholic Tradition, Current Trends, and the Truth*, the Père Marquette Lecture in Theology for 1989 (Milwaukee: Marquette University Press, 1989).

For a recent example of the attempt to link love and procreation to the marriage as a whole, while endorsing severing this bond in freely chosen acts of intimate union, see Lisa Sowle Cahill, "Can We Get Real About Sex?", in *Perspectives on Marriage: A Reader*, pp. 207–15.

[27] On this, see Charles E. Curran, "Divorce in the Light of a Revised Moral Theology", in his *Ongoing Revisions: Studies in Moral Theology* (Notre Dame, IN: University of Notre Dame Press, 1975), pp. 77–78.

this law."[28] Is it not true that today, in our contraceptive culture, chastity is considered obsolete, indeed, according to the ACLU, an unconstitutional imposition of religious doctrine, and that our youth are being instructed in the use of condoms and other contraceptive techniques?

It is no wonder that a recent survey of American males in their twenties and thirties showed that, at the time of the survey, they had a median average of 7.3 female sexual partners. For Catholic men in this age group, the median average was 6.9 female sexual partners. The overwhelming majority, over 70 percent, regularly used condoms to prevent contraception and the transmission of sexually transmitted "diseases".[29]

In addition, as Paul VI also foresaw, acceptance of contraception *and the rationale given to justify it* quickly leads to marital infidelity, because it is reasonable to fear that "husbands who become accustomed to contraceptive practices will lose respect for their wives [and will come] to disregard their wife's psychological and physical equilibrium and use their wives as instruments for serving their own desires. Consequently they will no longer view their wives as companions who should be treated with attentiveness and love."[30] The fear expressed by Paul has surely come to pass. It is no accident, as researchers such as Robert T. Michael have noted, that a dramatic increase in divorce in our society accompanied the dramatic increase in the practice of contraception, practiced both by fornicating couples prior to marriage and by husbands and wives in marriage.[31]

Moreover, as Paul VI again warned, acceptance of contraception and its underlying ideology has put a "dangerous power" into "the hands of rulers who care little about the moral law. Would anyone blame those in the highest offices of the state for employing a solution [contraception] morally permissible for spouses

[28] Paul VI, *Humanae vitae*, no. 17; Smith trans., p. 286.

[29] See *The Washington Post*, Thursday, April 15, 1993, sec. A, pp. 1, 16, for a summary of this recent survey of sexual habits of American males.

[30] Paul VI, *Humanae vitae*, no. 17; Smith trans., pp. 285–86.

[31] Robert T. Michael, "Why Did the U.S. Divorce Rate Double within a Decade?", in *Research in Population* (1988), pp. 361–99.

seeking to solve a family difficulty, when they strive to solve certain difficulties facing the whole nation?"[32] Is it not true that today we find State authorities resorting to enforced sterilization and the implanting of such contraceptive-abortifacient devices as Norplant in order to cope with serious social problems? And this is true not only of India and China but of many places in the United States.

Indeed, since contraception is an anti-life kind of act, it leads logically and inevitably to abortion as a backup for contraception, and State authorities have not been adverse to compulsory abortion, as the situation in China makes evident.

Truly, Paul VI is a prophet and *Humanae vitae* a prophetic document.

Conclusion: Two Contradictory Visions of Human Persons

Champions of contraception, in particular revisionist theologians like Louis Janssens, Charles Curran, and others, regularly claim that the "integral vision" of *Humanae vitae* is "physicalistic" and that in its place they are developing a truly "personalistic" vision of human persons and human sexuality.[33]

The truth is that we are confronted by two different kinds of "personalism", for, as John Paul II has perceptively noted, the anthropologies upon which the "integral vision" of Paul VI and the "disintegrative vision" of the champions of contraception rest present us with "irreconcilable concepts of the human person and of human sexuality".[34]

Paul VI's "integral vision", the vision constantly kept before our eyes by the Church, holds that human persons are *bodily*

[32] Paul VI, *Humanae vitae,* no. 17; Smith trans., p. 286.

[33] See the following: Louis Janssens, "Considerations on *Humanae Vitae*", *Louvain Studies* 2 (1969): 231–53; "Norms and Priorities in a Love Ethic", *Louvain Studies* 6 (1977): 207–38; Charles Curran, "Sexual Ethics: A Critique", in his *Issues in Sexual and Medical Ethics* (Notre Dame, Ind.: University of Notre Dame Press, 1978), pp. 30–51. See also Kosnik et al., op cit.

[34] John Paul II, *Familiaris consortio,* no. 32.

beings. When God created man, he did not create a "conscious subject" to whom he then, as an afterthought, gave a body. Rather, in creating man, "male and female he created them" (Gen 1:27)—that is, as bodily, sexual beings. Moreover, when God the Son became man, he became *flesh* (*sarx egeneto;* Jn 1:14). Precisely because human persons are *bodily beings, body persons,* their sexuality, *including* its procreative power, "wondrously surpasses the endowments of lower forms of life".[35] According to this integral vision of the human person, a living human body is a person, and every living human body, born or preborn, consciously aware of itself or crippled by severe mental handicaps so that it is not capable of consciousness, is a *person,* a being of surpassing goodness. Bodily life, on this vision, is not a merely instrumental good *for* the person, merely a condition for higher personal values, but is itself integral to the person and thus a good *of* the person.

Far different is the "personalism" of those who accept the "disintegrative vision" underlying the acceptance and practice of contraception. According to this "personalism", as we have seen, the procreative (or "reproductive") aspect of our sexuality is, of itself, merely a biological given, which needs to be "assumed into the human sphere" in order to *become* truly human and personal.[36] According to this vision, human persons are, in essence, "subjectivities", that is, conscious selves aware of themselves as selves and capable of relating to other selves. Bodily life is a condition for personal life, and when personal life (that is, consciously experienced life) has been irretrievably lost or will never emerge because of severe brain damage, bodily life is no longer a good but, as one of the revisionist theologians puts it, "an excessive hardship".[37] In his magnificent Encyclical on certain fundamental questions concerning the Church's moral teaching, Pope John

[35] Vatican Council II, *Gaudium et spes,* no. 51; see also Paul VI, *Humanae vitae,* nos. 10, 13; John Paul II, *Familiaris consortio,* no. 11.

[36] See the Majority Report of the Papal Commission on Population, the Family, and Natality, *The Birth Control Debate,* p. 71.

[37] See Richard McCormick, "To Save or Let Die: The Dilemma of Modern Medicine", in *How Brave a New World?* (Garden City, NY: Doubleday, 1978), p. 347.

Paul II rightly repudiated this dualistic position, comparing it to "certain ancient errors [gnosticism, Manichaeanism] ... always opposed by the Church".[38]

According to the "disintegrative vision" of human persons, moreover, a marriage "dies" when there is no longer any consciously experienced love between the spouses. Thus, the marriage simply is no longer, and one can no longer attribute indissolubility to what is nonexistent, and the partners of this dead marriage are then free to marry again.[39] As Cardinal Joseph Ratzinger observed, commenting on this "vision" of personhood, this understanding of human persons is rooted in the uncritical acceptance of an anthropology that ignores the deeper dimensions of human life and experience, *limiting the real and important simply to whatever may be occupying conscious thinking and living at the present moment.*[40]

The dualistic understanding of human persons and human sexuality, so evident in this "disintegrative vision" of sex, love, and procreation, claims to liberate the person from biological laws in order to free him for the enjoyment of personal and interpersonal values. But in reality, as Germain Grisez points out, it "alienates the human person from his or her own bodily reality". He continues:

> Thus Christian moral thought must remain grounded in a sound anthropology which maintains the bodiliness of the person. Such moral thought sees personal biological, not merely generically animal biological, meaning and value in human sexuality. The bodies which become one flesh in sexual intercourse are persons; their unity in a certain sense forms a single person, the potential procreator from whom the personal, bodily reality of a new human individual flows in material, bodily, personal continuity. An attack on this biological process is

---

[38] Pope John Paul II, Encyclical *Veritatis splendor,* no. 49.

[39] On this, see Richard McCormick, S.J., "Notes on Moral Theology 1975", reprinted in *Notes on Moral Theology 1965–1980* (Washington, DC: University Press of America, 1980), pp. 544–60; Bernard Haering, "Internal Forum Solutions to Insoluble Marriage Cases", *The Jurist* 30 (1970): 22.

[40] Joseph Ratzinger, "Zur Frage nach der Unauflöslichkeit der Ehe", in *Ehe und Ehescheidung,* edited by F. Heinrich and E. Eid (Munich, 1972), pp. 49–50.

an attack on the personal value of life . . . in its moment of tradition.[41]

Truly Pope Paul is a prophet. He upholds the priceless truth that human beings are bodily persons and that there is indeed an intimate, unbreakable bond between sex, love, and procreation. He reminds us that every human person, born or unborn, ought to be wanted and loved and that babies are not things to be wanted or unwanted but God's gift, indeed, the supreme gift of marriage. It is time for men and women to shape their choices and actions in accord with the truth proclaimed in *Humanae vitae*.

[41] Germain Grisez, "Dualism and the New Morality", in *Atti del Congresso internazionale (Roma-Napoli, 17–24 aprile 1974): Tommaso D'Aquino nel suo settimo centenario*, vol. 5, *L'agire morale,* ed. M. Zalba (Napoli: Edizioni Domenicane Italiane, 1977): 329–30.

4

"Begotten, Not Made": Catholic Teaching on the Laboratory Generation of Human Life

Introduction

The first child to be born after being conceived *in vitro* and not in her mother's body was Louise Brown. It is paradoxical, in my opinion, that Louise was born on July 25, 1978, ten years to the day after Pope Paul VI's Encyclical *Humanae vitae* was promulgated. Louise's birth, indeed, her conception, would not have been possible had a technology separating "baby making" from "love making" not been developed. Yet a claim central to Pope Paul's Encyclical was that "there is an unbreakable bond [*nexu indissolubili*], established by God, which man is not permitted to break on his own initiative, between its unitive meaning and its procreative meaning.[1]

Pope Paul's concern in *Humanae vitae* was with contraception and not with the laboratory generation of human life. But his teaching on the "unbreakable bond" between the two meanings of the conjug..l act, as will be seen, plays a central role in the 1987 Instruction on Respect for Human Life in Its Origin and on the Dignity of Procreation —called *Donum vitae* in Latin—in which the Congregation for the Doctrine of the Faith formally addressed the moral issues raised by new reproductive technologies. This

---

[1] Pope Paul VI, Encyclical *Humanae vitae*, no. 12.

85

document, drawing on the understanding of marriage and human procreation found in the Catholic theological tradition, insists that the generation of human life, if it is to respect the dignity of both parents and children, "must be the fruit and sign of the mutual self-giving of the spouses, of their love and fidelity".[2]

In its treatment of heterologous fertilization, in which gametes, whether ova or sperm, from parties other than the spouses are used to generate new human life, the *Instruction*, not surprisingly, concludes that this way of generating human life is gravely immoral. It is so because such fertilization is "contrary to the unity of marriage, to the dignity of the spouses, to the vocation proper to parents, and the child's right to be conceived and brought into the world in marriage and through marriage".[3]

Although some find this judgment of the *Instruction* too restrictive of human freedom,[4] many people, Catholic and non-Catholic as well, can appreciate the reasons behind it, even if, in some highly unique situations, they might be ready to justify heterologous modes of generating human life. Nonetheless, they recognize that when a man and a woman marry, they "give" themselves exclusively to each other and that the "selves" they give are sexual and procreative beings. Just as they violate their marital commit-

---

[2] Congregation for the Doctrine of the Faith, *Instruction on Respect for Human Life in Its Origin and the Dignity of Procreation*, pt. 2, A, 1, with a footnote reference to Vatican Council II, *Gaudium et spes*, no. 50. The English text has been printed in pamphlet form by Ignatius Press, San Francisco (1987), and all references here will be to this edition. The material cited in the text is found on p. 22 of this edition.

[3] Ibid., pt. 2, A, 2 (p. 23), with a footnote reference to Pope Pius XII, Discourse to Those Taking Part in the Fourth International Congress of Catholic Doctors, September 29, 1949, AAS 41 (1949): 559.

[4] It should be noted that many people, particularly in affluent Western democracies such as the United States, where contraception has become a way of life, are favorably disposed to the use of heterologous insemination and fertilization to help a childless couple have a baby, at least in some way, "of their own". Some, in fact, see the artificial generation of human life as "more human" than the "reproductive roulette" of generating children through sexual coition. See, for instance, Joseph Fletcher, *The Ethics of Genetic Control: Ending Reproductive Roulette* (Garden City, NY: Doubleday Anchor Books, 1972).

ment by attempting, after marriage, to "give" themselves to another in sexual union, so too they dishonor their marital covenant by freely choosing to exercise their procreative powers with someone other than their spouse, the person to whom they have given themselves, including their power to procreate, "forswearing all others".

But many of these same people, Catholic as well as non-Catholic, find the *Instruction*'s teaching on the immorality of the "simple case" of *in vitro* fertilization and embryo transfer a different matter. In this case, there is no use of gametic materials from third parties; the child conceived is genetically the child of husband and wife, who are and will remain its parents. In this case, there need be no deliberate creation of "excess" human lives that will be discarded (perhaps through a procedure that some euphemistically call "pregnancy reduction"),[5] frozen, or made the objects of medical experimentations of no benefit to them. In this case there need be no intention to monitor the developing child *in utero* with a view toward its abortion should it develop some abnormality. Nor need there even be, in this case, the use of masturbation—a means judged intrinsically immoral by the Catholic Magisterium—in order to obtain the father's sperm, for his sperm can be retrieved in nonmasturbatory ways. In this case, there is, apparently, only the intent to use modern technology as a means of helping a married couple, unable either by reason of the wife's blocked fallopian tubes or the husband's low sperm production or other causes, to have a child of their own and give it a home where it can take root and grow under the loving tutelage of its own parents. Many people, including several Catholic theologians, believe that recourse to *in vitro* fertilization and embryo transfer in this "simple case" is fully legitimate, since it does not

[5] "Pregnancy reduction" is the expression used by some doctors who deliberately kill within the womb "excess" children who have been conceived *in vitro* and implanted in their mother's wombs to enhance the likelihood that at least one child will survive pregnancy. Should all the embryos implanted continue development, and since multiple pregnancies raise some serious problems, the choice is made to resolve these problems by killing off excess and hence unwanted children.

seem to violate any one's rights but, to the contrary, seems to help a married couple's love blossom into life. They quite reasonably ask what is morally offensive here? What evil is being willed and done? Is not the Magisterium of the Church being too rigoristic here? Is it not insensitive to the agony experienced by involuntarily sterile married couples who are simply seeking to realize one of the goods of marriage by making intelligent use of modern technology?

Here I will first present the principles set forth in the *Instruction* to support its conclusions. Since the *Instruction* does not, in general, seek to establish the truth of these principles or show their special place within the Christian view of human life, I will then attempt to show their truth and reasonableness.[6] Finally, I will consider some objections, raised by Catholic theologians, against the position taken by the *Instruction* on homologous *in vitro* fertilization and embryo transfer.

---

[6] Joseph Boyle, Jr., has written "An Introduction to the Vatican Instruction on Reproductive Technologies", *Linacre Quarterly* 55 (July 1988): 20–28; reprinted as "An Overview of the Vatican's Instruction on Reproductive Ethics" in *The Gift of Life: The Proceedings of a National Conference on the Vatican Instruction on Reproductive Ethics and Technology,* ed. Marilyn Wallace, R.S.M., and Thomas W. Hilgers, M.D. (Omaha, NE: Pope Paul VI Institute Press, 1990), pp. 19–26. References are to Boyle's work as reprinted in *The Gift of Life.* Boyle says that the most important principles underlying the *Instruction*'s teaching can be expressed as five propositions. "First, God makes human individuals in His own image and likeness, and He is directly involved in the coming-to-be of each new person. Second, the human person is one being, bodily as well as spiritual, so bodily life and sexuality may not be treated as mere means to more fundamental purposes. Third, every living human individual, from the moment of conception, should be treated with the full respect due a person and so is inviolable. A human being is always a he or she, an I or a you, never an object, a mere something. Fourth, sexual activity and procreation can be morally good only if they are part of marital intercourse. Fifth, in marital intercourse, love-making and life-giving should not be separated" (p. 20). Boyle observes that in general the *Instruction* does not attempt to establish these principles, although it does provide some argumentation to support the principle requiring that all human individuals be treated as persons from the moment of conception (p. 21).

The Reasoning of the *Instruction*

The *Instruction* presents three principal lines of reasoning to support its conclusion that married couples ought not resort to *in vitro* fertilization and embryo transfer, even when the ovum comes from the mother and the sperm used to fertilize it are retrieved in a morally acceptable way from her husband.

The first line of reasoning appeals to the "inseparability principle" that, as we have seen, is at the heart of Pope Paul's *Humanae vitae*. Applying this teaching to the issue of homologous artificial fertilization, the "simple case" with which we are concerned, the *Instruction* affirms, with Pope Pius XII, that "it is never permitted to separate these different aspects to such a degree as positively to exclude either the procreative intention [as is done in contraception] or the conjugal relation."[7] "Thus," the *Instruction* concludes,

> fertilization is licitly sought when it is the result of a "conjugal act which is *per se* suitable for the generation of children to which marriage is ordered by its very nature and by which the spouses become one flesh". But from the moral point of view procreation is deprived of its proper perfection when it is not desired as the fruit of the conjugal act, that is to say, of the specific act of the spouses' union.[8]

According to this line of reasoning, it is morally wrong for married couples to generate human life outside the marital act, because to do so is to choose to sever the bond between the unitive and procreative meanings of the conjugal act. But a willingness to do this, apparently, entails a willingness to deprive procreation of the goodness that it is meant to have as the fruit of the conjugal act.

[7] *Instruction*, 2, B, 4, a (p. 26), citing Pius XII, "Discourse to Those Taking Part in the Second Naples World Congress on Fertility and Human Sterility", May 19, 1956, AAS 48 (1956): 470.

[8] Ibid., 2, B, 4, a (p. 26; emphasis in original document omitted). The internal citation is to the *Code of Canon Law*, can. 1061.

A second argument presented in the *Instruction* to support its conclusion on the immorality of homologous *in vitro* fertilization and embryo transfer is based on the dignity of the child so conceived. The Vatican document insists that the child "cannot be desired or conceived as the product of an intervention of medical or biological techniques", inasmuch as "that would be the equivalent of reducing him to an object of scientific technology. No one may subject the coming of a child into the world to conditions of technical efficacy which are to be evaluated according to standards of control and dominion."[9] But, the *Instruction* continues,

> [C]onception *in vitro* is the result of the technical action which presides over fertilization. Such fertilization is neither in fact achieved nor positively willed as the expression and fruit of a specific act of the conjugal union. In homologous IVF and ET, therefore, even if it is considered in the context of *de facto* existing sexual relations, the generation of the human person is objectively deprived of its proper perfection, namely, that of being the result and fruit of a conjugal act in which the spouses can become "cooperators with God for giving life to a new person".[10]

The line of reasoning here can be summed up as follows: to desire to cause a child as a product of a technique is to make the child an object. But this is not compatible with the equality in personal dignity between the child and those who give it life.

A third line of reasoning is also given in the *Instruction* to support its conclusion. This line of reasoning is based on the "language of the body". According to the *Instruction*,

> spouses mutually express their personal love in the "language of the body", which clearly involves both "spousal meanings" and parental ones. The conjugal act by which the couple mutually express their self-gift at the same time expresses openness to the

[9] Ibid., 2, B, 4, c (p. 27).

[10] Ibid., 2, B, 5 (p. 29; emphasis in original omitted); the internal reference is to John Paul II, Apostolic Exhortation *Familiaris consortio*, no. 14; AAS 74 (1982): 96.

gift of life. It is an act that is inseparably corporal and spiritual. It is in their bodies and through their bodies that the spouses consummate their marriage and are able to become fathers and mothers.[11]

The document then concludes,

> In order to respect the language of their bodies and of their natural generosity, the conjugal union must take place with respect for its openness to procreation, and the procreation of a person must be the fruit and result of married love. The origin of the human being thus follows from a procreation that is "linked to the union, not only biological but also spiritual, of the parents, made one by the bond of marriage". Fertilization achieved outside the bodies of the couple remains by this very fact deprived of the meanings and values which are expressed in the language of the body and in the union of married persons.[12]

According to this line of reasoning, *in vitro* fertilization, which occurs outside the body of the mother and independently of the bodily act by which spouses express their marital union in a unique and spousal way, is a way of generating human life that fails to respect the "language of the body". It is a mode of human generation that in no way acknowledges the deep human significance of the personal gift, bodily and spiritual in nature, of husband and wife to one another in the marital act.

It seems to me that the argument based on the "language of the body", one central to the "theology of the body" set forth by Pope John Paul II so extensively,[13] is intimately linked to the argument based on the "inseparability principle". Consequently, in what follows I will seek to show how these two lines of reasoning seem

---

[11] Ibid., 2, B, 4, b (pp. 26–27; emphasis in the original omitted), with a footnote reference to Pope John Paul II, General Audience of January 16, 1980; *Insegnamenti di Giovanni Paolo II* 3:1 (1980): 148–52.

[12] Ibid. (p. 27); the internal citation is from Pope John Paul II, "Discourse to Those Taking Part in the 35th General Assembly of the World Medical Association", October 29, 1983; AAS 76 (1984): 393.

[13] See his *Original Unity of Man and Woman: Catechesis on Genesis* (Boston: St. Paul Editions, 1981).

to merge and how closely they depend on a fundamental vision of marriage, the marital act, and the generation of human life.

Of the three lines of reasoning found in the *Instruction* to support its conclusion, I believe that the second, which rejects *in vitro* fertilization and embryo transfer on the grounds that generating human life in the laboratory is a form of production and demeans human life by treating it as if it were a product, provides the basis for the most straightforward argument against resorting to the laboratory generation of human life. Still the other two lines of reasoning, in my opinion, illumine the wider issues concerning human existence raised by new reproductive technologies. But to appreciate these lines of reasoning, it is first necessary to probe the meaning of marriage and the relationship between marriage, the marital act, and the generation of human life.

Marital Rights and Capabilities, the Marital Act, and the Generation of Human Life

This subject was taken up in Chapter One, and thus only a summary exposition will be given here. The principal truth is that husbands and wives, precisely because they have given themselves irrevocably to one another in marriage, have capacitated themselves, i.e., made themselves *fit,* to do what married persons are supposed to do, namely, to give one another a special kind of love, spousal or conjugal love, to express that love in the marital act, and to welcome the gift of new human life and give it the home where it can take root and grow. In sharp contrast to the genital act of fornicators and adulterers, which in no way unites two irreplaceable and nonsubstitutable spouses but simply joins two individuals who are in principle replaceable and substitutable — disposable — the marital act of husbands and wives unites two persons who have made each other irreplaceable and nonsubstitutable. Precisely because they are irrevocably committed to one another, husbands and wives have also rendered themselves fit to welcome human life lovingly, nourish it humanely, and educate it in the love and service of God and neighbor.[14] They have, in short, given themselves the capacity to be parents, mothers and fathers, of new human persons.

The marital act, as we have seen, is more than a simple genital act between a man and a woman who merely *happen* to be married. Precisely as *marital,* it is an act that inwardly participates in the marriage and is thus open to the "goods" or "blessings" of marriage, that is, the good of steadfast fidelity and exclusive marital love and the good of children. It is, in short an act open to (1) the communication of spousal love and (2) the reception of new human life. Were a husband or wife deliberately to choose to "close" their genital union to either of these great goods of marriage, they would make their freely chosen genital activity to be something other than a true marital act, as Paul VI perceptively indicated in *Humanae vitae.*[15]

The marital act, in other words, is by its own inner nature love-giving or unitive and open to the transmission of human life or procreative. And it is so precisely because it is *marital,* that is, an act participating in marriage and the goods perfective of it. The bond, therefore, that unites the two meanings of the marital act is the marriage itself. But "what God has joined together, let no man put asunder." It is for this reason, I believe, that there is an

[14] I have sought to defend the truth of this claim elsewhere. See, for instance, my *Sex, Marriage, and Chastity: Reflections of a Catholic Layman, Spouse, and Parent* (Chicago: Franciscan Herald Press, 1981), chap. 5; "Sexual Ethics and Human Dignity", in *Persona, verità e morale: Atti del Congresso internazionale di teologia morale (Roma, 7–12 aprile 1986)* (Rome: Città Nuova Editrice, 1988), pp. 477–95, in particular, pp. 488–89.

[15] Paul VI suggested this in *Humanae vitae,* no. 13. There he explicitly said that a "conjugal act", obviously using this expression in a purely descriptive sense to designate a genital act between a man and a woman who happen to be married, is recognized by everyone as contrary to the right moral order if imposed by one of the spouses on the other against the other's reasonable desires and condition. Similarly, he continued, it should be recognized that a "conjugal act", again using the expression in a purely descriptive sense, that impairs this act's capacity to bring forth new life is contrary to the Creator's design and plan.

"unbreakable connection between the unitive meaning and the procreative meaning" of the conjugal act.

The marital act is not, as Pope Pius XII rightly said, "a mere organic function for the transmission of the germs of life". It is rather, as he noted, "a personal action, a simultaneous natural self-giving which, in the words of Holy Scripture, effects the union in 'one flesh' . . . [and] implies a personal cooperation [of the spouses with God in giving new human life]."[16] Indeed, as Pope Paul VI put it, "because of its intrinsic nature [*intimam rationem*] the conjugal act, while uniting husband and wife in the most intimate of bonds, also makes them *fit* [*eos idoneos etiam facit*] to bring forth new life."[17]

In addition, one can rightly say that the marital act speaks the "language of the body". It beautifully expresses the personal, bodily integrity of the spouses. To see what this means, I think that some observations by John Finnis concerning personal integrity are relevant. According to Finnis,

> personal integrity involves . . . that one be reaching out with one's will, that is, freely choosing, real goods, and that one's efforts to realize these goods involves, where appropriate, one's bodily activity, so that that activity is as much the constitutive subject of what one does as one's act of choice is. That one really be realizing goods in the world; that one be doing so by one's free and aware choice, that that choice be carried into effect by one's own bodily action, including, where appropriate, bodily acts of communication and cooperation with other real people — these are the fundamental aspects of personal integrity.[18]

In the marital act, a husband and wife are indeed freely choosing and realizing real goods in the world — their own marital union and new human life; their bodily activity is surely a constitutive

---

[16] Pope Pius XII, "Apostolate of the Midwives: An Address to the Italian Catholic Union of Midwives", October 29, 1951; text in *The Catholic Mind* 50 (1952): 61.

[17] Pope Paul VI, *Humanae vitae*, no. 12.

[18] John Finnis, "Personal Integrity, Sexual Morality, and Responsible Parenthood", *Anthropos* (now *Anthropotes*) 1, 1 (1985), p. 46.

subject of what they do; and cooperation with another is not only appropriate but necessary. The marital act is an utterly unique kind of human act; it is a collaborate, personal act carrying out the choice of the spouses to actualize their marriage and participate in the goods perfective of it.

Procreation vs. Reproduction

As we have just seen, when human life is given through the act of marital union, it comes, even when it is ardently desired, as a "gift" crowning the act itself. The marital act is not an act of "making", either babies or love. Love is not a product that one makes; it is a gift that one gives—the gift of self. Similarly, a baby is not a product inferior to its producers; it is, rather, a being equal in dignity to its parents. The marital act is surely something that husbands and wives "do"; it is not something that they "make". But what is the difference between "making" and "doing", and what bearing does this difference have on the issue of *in vitro* fertilization and embryo transfer?

In "making", the action proceeds from an agent or agents to something in the external world, to a product. Autoworkers, for instance, produce cars; cooks produce meals; bakers make cakes, and so on. Such action is transitive in nature because it passes from the acting subject(s) to an object fashioned by him (or them) and external to them. In making, which is governed by the rules of art, interest centers on the product made—and ordinarily products that do not measure up to standards are discarded; at any rate, "defective". Those who produce the products may be morally good autoworkers or bakers or cooks, or they may be morally bad, but our interest in "making" is in the product, not the producers, and we would prefer to have good cakes made by morally bad bakers than indigestible ones baked by saints who are incompetent bakers.

In "doing", the action abides in the acting subject(s). The action is immanent and is governed by the requirements of prudence, not art. If the action is morally good, it perfects the agent; if bad, it degrades and dehumanizes him.[19] It must be noted, moreover, that every act of making is also a doing insofar as it is freely chosen, for the choice to make something is something that we "do", and this choice, as self-determining, abides in us. Thus, in choosing to make a cake for someone's birthday, one is choosing to enhance the good of human friendship and is "doing" something good and making oneself to be, in this respect, a good person. Likewise, in choosing to make pornographic films, one is choosing to do something evil because it dishonors the dignity of human persons. There are, in other words, some things that we ought not to make, because choosing to make them is morally bad.

The marital act, as we have seen, is not an act of making. It is rather an act freely chosen by spouses to express their marital union, one open to the communication of marital love and to the transmission of human life. As such, the marital act is an act inwardly perfective of them and of their life as spouses, the life of which they are cosubjects, just as they are the cosubjects of the marital act itself. Even when they choose this act with the ardent hope that, through it, new human life will be given to them, the life begotten is not the product of their act but is a "gift superven-ing on and giving permanent embodiment to" the marital act itself.[20] When human life comes to be through the marital act, we can say quite properly that the spouses are "begetting" or "pro-creating". They are not "making" anything. The life they receive is "begotten, not made".

But when human life comes to be as a result of *in vitro* fertilization— whether heterologous or homologous—it is the end product of a series of actions, transitive in nature, undertaken by different persons. The spouses "produce" the gametic materials which others then use in order to make the final product, the

[19] Classic sources for the distinction between making and doing are: Aristotle, *Metaphysics*, bk. 9, c. 8, 1050a23–1050b1; St. Thomas Aquinas, *In IX Metaphysicorum*, lect. 8, no. 1865, *Summa theologiae*, 1, 4, 2, ad 2; 1, 14, 5, ad 1; 1, 181, 1.

[20] Catholic Bishops Committee on Bioethical Issues, *In Vitro Fertilization: Moral-ity and Public Policy* (London: Catholic Information Services, 1983), no. 23.

child. In such a procedure the child "comes into existence, not as a gift supervening on an act expressive of the marital union . . . but rather in the manner of a product of a making (and, typically, as the end product of a process managed and carried out by persons other than his parents)."[21] The life generated is "made", not "begotten".

But a child is not a product inferior to its producers and subject to quality controls (even if the choice is made not to apply these controls). It is, rather, as I have noted already, a person equal in dignity to its parents. A child, therefore, ought not to be treated as if it were a product. A child, therefore, ought not to be generated by *in vitro* fertilization, heterologous or homologous.

Advocates of homologous *in vitro* fertilization, including some Catholic theologians, reject this line of reasoning. As Richard McCormick says, "They do not see IVF as 'manufacture' of a 'product'. Fertilization *happens* when sperm and egg are brought together in a petri dish. The technician's 'intervention is a condition for its happening; it is not a cause.' "[22] Moreover, McCormick continues, "the attitudes of the parents and the technicians can be every bit as reverential and respectful as they would be in the face of human life naturally conceived."[23] Indeed, in McCormick's view (and in that of some other writers), homologous *in vitro* fertilization and embryo transfer can be considered an "extension" of intercourse, so that the child generated can still be regarded as the "fruit" of the spouses' love. While it is preferable, if possible, to generate the baby through the marital act, it is, in the cases we are concerned with, impossible to do so. Given the concrete situation, any disadvantages inherent in the generation of human lives apart from the marital act are clearly counterbalanced by the great good of new human lives and the fulfillment of the desire for children of couples who otherwise cannot have them. In this concrete

[21] Ibid., no. 24.

[22] Richard A. McCormick, S.J., *The Critical Calling: Reflections on Moral Dilemmas since Vatican II* (Washington, DC: Georgetown University Press, 1989), p. 337; the internal citation is from William Daniel, S.J., "In Vitro Fertilization: Two Problem Areas", *Australasian Catholic Record* 63 (1986): 27.

[23] Ibid.

situation, it is not unrealistic, so this line of thinking holds, to say that IVF is simply a way of "extending" the marital act.

Naturally, those who choose to produce a baby make that choice only as a means to an ulterior end. They may well intend that the baby be received into an authentic child-parent relationship, in which he will live in the communion which befits those who share personal dignity. If realized, this intended end for the sake of which the choice is made to produce the baby will be good for the baby as well as for the parents. But, even so, and despite McCormick's claim to the contrary, the baby's initial status is the status of a product. In *in vitro* fertilization, the technician does not simply assist the marital act (that would be licit), but, as Benedict Ashley rightly notes, "*substitutes* for that act of personal relationship and communication one which is like a chemist making a compound or a gardener planting a seed. The technician has thus become the principal cause of generation, acting through the instrumental forces of sperm and ovum."[24] Moreover, the claim that *in vitro* fertilization is an "extension" of the marital act and not a substitution for it is simply contrary to fact. "What is extended", as Ashley also notes, "is not the act of intercourse, but the intention: from an intention to beget a child naturally to getting it by IVF, by artificial insemination, or by help of a surrogate mother."[25]

Since the child's initial status in *in vitro* fertilization is that of a product, its status is subpersonal. Thus, the choice to produce a baby is inevitably the choice to enter into a relationship with the baby considered, not as an equal, but as a product inferior to its producers. But this initial relationship of those who choose to produce babies with the babies they produce is inconsistent with and so impedes the communion of persons endowed with equal dignity which is appropriate to any interpersonal relationship. It is the choice of a bad means to a good end. Moreover, in producing babies, if the product is defective, a new person comes to be as

[24] Benedict Ashley, O.P., "The Chill Factor in Moral Theology", *Linacre Quarterly* 57, no. 4 (November 1990): 71.

[25] Ibid., p. 72.

unwanted. Thus, those who produce babies not only choose life for some but—does anyone doubt it?—quietly dispose of at least some of those who are not developing normally.[26]

In short, human beings, who are the created words that the uncreated Word of God became and is, ought, like the uncreated Word, to "be begotten, not made". They are begotten in the marital act, a unique human act expressive of the marital union of husbands and wives and open to the generation of new human life; they are made in laboratories by *in vitro* fertilization, whether heterologous or homologous. Begetting is a personal act that, by its nature, cannot be "delegated" to others. Spouses can no more delegate to others the privilege they have of begetting human life than they can delegate to others the right they have to engage in the marital act.[27]

[26] In the previous paragraphs, in addition to citing from Benedict Ashley, I have also paraphrased material developed by Germain Grisez, John Finnis, Joseph Boyle, and William E. May, " 'Every Marital Act Ought to Be Open to New Life: Toward a Clearer Understanding", *Thomist* 52 (1988): 365–426; reprinted in the book by the same authors and John Ford, S.J., *The Teaching of "Humanae Vitae": A Defense* (San Francisco: Ignatius Press, 1988).

[27] On this, see the thought-provoking comments of Janet Smith in her essay, "The Vocation of Christian Marriage as an Approach to the Bioethics of Human Reproduction", in *The Gift of Life,* pp. 49–60, at pp. 58–59.

The *Catechism of the Catholic Church* contains a brief but excellent section on the laboratory reproduction of human life (nos. 2376–78, pp. 571–772). This document quite rightly affirms: "A child is not something owed to one, but is a *gift.* The 'supreme gift of marriage' is a human person. A child may not be considered a piece of property, an idea to which an alleged 'right to a child' would lead. In this area, only the child possesses genuine rights: the right 'to be the fruit of the specific act of the conjugal love of his parents,' and 'the right to be respected as a person from the moment of his conception' [*Donum vitae,* II, 8]" (no. 2378).

5

The Christian Family: A Domestic Church

One of the most remarkable and important documents of the Magisterium since Vatican Council II is Pope John Paul II's Apostolic Exhortation on the role of the Christian family in the modern world, *Familiaris consortio*.[1] He has himself described the Exhortation as "a *summa* of the teaching of the Church on the life, the tasks, the responsibilities, and the mission of marriage and of the family in the world today".[2] Part three of this document, "The Role of the Christian Family", considers the mission that the

---

[1] For a bibliography, see *La familiaris consortio* (Vatican City: Libreria Editrice Vaticana, 1982). For commentaries, see the special issue of *Divinitas* 26, no. 3 (1982): 247–76, "L'exortazione apostolica *Familiaris consortio* commentata da teologi di varie nazioni". Of special relevance to the themes of this paper, in my opinion, are the essays by Ramón García de Haro, "El matrimonio, comunidad de amor, al servicio de la vida", pp. 332–49, and Jean-Marie Aubert, "La Famille cellule d'Église". See also Augusto Sarmiento, *A missao de familia christa (Commentarios a exortacao apostolica Familiaris consortio)* (Braga: Ed. Theologica, 1985), and *Pope John Paul II and the Family*, ed. Michael Wrenn (Chicago: Franciscan Herald Press, 1983). Of the essays in the Wrenn collection, the more relevant are Joseph M. Boyle, Jr., "The Role of the Christian Family, Articles 17–27", pp. 49–72; William E. May, "The Role of the Christian Family, Articles 49–58", pp. 167–92, and Robert Levis, "The Role of the Christian Family, Articles 59–64", pp. 193–207.

[2] John Paul II, Address of December 22, 1981, in which the Pope presented his new Apostolic Exhortation. The text is found in *Enchiridion familiae: Textos del Magistero pontificio y conciliar sobre el matrimonio y la familia (siglos I a XX)*, ed. Augusto Sarmiento and Javier Escriva Ivars (Madrid: Ediciones Rialp, 1992). Six volumes, 4:3415.

family is called to exercise, in virtue of its very being, in the world today (*Familiaris consortio*, no. 17). The Holy Father identifies four principal tasks of the Christian family: to form a community of persons (nos. 18–27), to serve life (nos. 28–41), to participate in the development of society (nos. 42–48), and to share in the life and mission of the Church (nos. 49–64).

My purpose here is to reflect on some of the major themes taken up by John Paul II in his analysis of the role of the Christian family in the life and mission of the Church. His teaching can be summarized as follows: The Christian family shares in the saving mission of the Church, with an original and characteristic task, linked to its very nature. Because of this, the family can be called the "domestic Church", a living image of the very mystery of the Spouse of Christ. As such, it is called to participate in the three-fold mission of Christ as Prophet, Priest, and King. It shares in the prophetic mission of Christ by being a believing and evangelizing community, in his priestly mission by being a community in dialogue with God, and in his kingly mission by being a community at the service of mankind.[3]

Because the Holy Father's teaching on this issue is so rich and cannot be briefly examined in an adequate way, I have therefore selected the following themes on which to focus attention: (1) the foundation of the Christian family's specific and original role in the Church: its identity as the "Church in miniature"; (2) the dynamic source of the Christian family's saving mission in the Church and for the Church: Christian conjugal love; and (3) the substantive content of its mission: participation in the prophetic, priestly, and kingly roles of Christ.

---

[3] The *Catechism of the Catholic Church*, neatly summarizing the teaching of Vatican Council II and Pope John Paul II, discusses the Christian family, rooted in the marriage of one man and one woman, as the domestic Church in two places: first, in the chapter devoted to the sacrament of marriage in pt. 2, nos. 1655–58, and second, in its discussion of the Christian family in the chapter on the Fourth Commandment in pt. 3, nos. 2204–6.

1. The Foundation of the Christian Family's Specific and Original Role in the Church: Its Identity as the "Church in Miniature"

At the very beginning of part three of *Familiaris consortio,* John Paul II stresses that the family must become what it *is.*[4] He writes as follows:

> The family finds in the plan of God the Creator and Redeemer not only its *identity,* what it *is,* but also its *mission,* what it can and should *do.* The role that God calls the family to perform in history derives from what the family is; its role represents the dynamic and existential development of what it is. Each family finds within itself a summons that cannot be ignored, and that specifies both its dignity and its responsibility: family, *become* what you *are* (no. 17).

The mission of the family, in other words, is its vocation, the role it should fulfill, the tasks it should carry out. And this vocation, this role, these tasks are rooted in the family's *being* the sort or kind of reality that it is according to the plan of God, the Creator and Redeemer.

We can begin with the plan of God the Creator. The specific identity of the family as such, whether Christian or not, is established at the beginning by God's creative act, for God is the author of marriage, who has given to it, as Pius XI so well said, "the ends for which it was instituted, the laws that govern it, and the blessings that flow from it".[5] And in God's plan the family is

---

[4] In stressing that human persons must become what they *are* and that the family must become what it *is,* John Paul II takes up a profoundly biblical theme, one developed particularly by St. Paul. On the Pauline development of this theme, see George T. Montague, S.M., *Maturing in Christ: St. Paul's Program for Christian Growth* (Milwaukee: Bruce Publishing, 1962).

[5] Pius XI, Encyclical *Casti connubii,* no. 10; *Enchiridion familiae* (hereafter EF) 1:715. That God is the author of marriage is the clear teaching of Genesis 1 and 2. On this see Edward Schillebeeckx, O.P., *Marriage: Human Reality and Saving Mystery* (New York: Sheed & Ward, 1965), pp. 11–27; Peter Elliott, *What God Has Joined: The Sacramentality of Marriage* (New York: Alba House, 1990), pp. 6–9. This is also the firm and constant teaching of the Church. See Council of Florence, *Decree for*

established, in the words of Vatican Council II, as an "intimate community of life and love".[6] In other words, both the essence and the role of the family are specified by love. "Hence," as John Paul says, "the family has *the mission to guard, reveal and communicate love*" (no. 17).

It is remarkable, but not surprising, that John Paul II here defines the essence and role of the family in terms of what he had earlier affirmed to be "the fundamental and innate vocation of *every* human being", that is, to *love* (no. 11). For, as Joseph Boyle has observed, "although some [human persons] are called to live out their vocation outside of married life—as religious or priests or in the single state—all of us are members of families, and it is within this context that the call of the vocation to love is understood and accepted. In short, the specific mission of the family is to nourish and promote in a very special way the most important thing in life: love."[7]

The mission to guard, reveal, and communicate love is entrusted to *every* human family, whether Christian or not, by virtue of its very being as a reality having God as its author, who even prior to his revelation of himself in Christ used the marriage of man and woman and the family based on this union as an image of his loving union with his people (cf. Hos 1–3). Marriage, in short, by virtue of being a human reality with God as its author, is a fitting sign of the covenant of life and love God wills to exist between himself and his people; that is, marriage is of its very nature a reality pointing to something beyond itself—the love-giving, life-giving union of God and mankind.

But an even greater mission has been entrusted to the *Christian*

Armenians, EF, 1:137–38; Council of Trent, Session 24, Decree *De doctrina sacramenti matrimonii*, EF, 1:142–53 and canon 1, EF, 1:144–46; Pius VI, Letter *Deessemus nobis*, September 16, 1788, EF, 1:312; Leo XIII, *Inscrutabili*, April 24, 1878, EF, 1:312; Leo XIII, Encyclical *Arcanum divinae sapientiae*, February 10, 1880, EF, 1:481–84; Pius XI, Encyclical *Casti connubii*, December 31, 1930, EF, 1:712–13; Vatican Council II, Pastoral Constitution *Gaudium et spes*, no. 48, EF, 3:1830; Paul VI, Encyclical *Humanae vitae*, July 25, 1968, no. 8, EF, 3:1913; John Paul II, Apostolic Exhortation *Familiaris consortio*, no. 11, EF, 3217–18.

[6] Vatican Council II, *Gaudium et spes*, no. 48.

[7] Boyle, pp. 50–51.

family according to the plan of God the Redeemer. For we must remember that we are sinners in need of redemption. Because of sin, man finds himself, as the Fathers of Vatican Council II noted, "divided within himself", with the result that "the whole life of men, both individual and social, shows itself to be a struggle, and a dramatic one, between good and evil, light and darkness. Man finds that he is unable of himself to overcome the assaults of evil successfully. . . . But the Lord himself came to free and strengthen man, renewing him inwardly and casting out the 'prince of this world' (Jn 12:31) who held him in the bondage of sin" (*Gaudium et spes,* no. 13). He has sent us his Son as our savior and redeemer. In fact, it is only through Jesus that, as Vatican Council II teaches and as John Paul II reminds us time and time again, "man is fully revealed to himself".[8] And Christ the Redeemer not only recreates human persons and reveals to them their fullest identity, he also recreates marriage and family and in doing so reveals their fullest identity.

The family, as *Christian,* finds its origin, inner identity, and vocation in Christ and his Bride, the Church. For it is the Church, as John Paul writes, that both "gives birth to . . . the Christian family" and, "by proclaiming the word of God . . . , reveals to the Christian family its true identity, what it is and what it should be according to the Lord's plan" (no. 49). Since the reality of the Christian family derives from its being generated by the Church, the identity of the Christian family is that of a "Church in miniature" (no. 49), summoned to "imitate and relive the same self-giving and sacrificial love that the Lord Jesus has for the entire human race", that is, a redemptive, grace-giving kind of love (no. 49). The Christian family thus participates in the very mystery of the Church.

Properly to understand what this means, however, it is necessary to consider how the Church as mother "gives birth" to the Christian family. And to understand this we need to consider the relationship between baptism and marriage.

The family is rooted in marriage. But marriage, as the Church

---

[8] See Vatican Council II, *Gaudium et spes,* no. 22: "Christ the Lord, the new Adam, in the very revelation of the mystery of the Father and of his love, fully reveals man to himself and brings to light his most high calling." See John Paul II, Encyclical *Redemptor hominis,* no. 22, Encyclical *Veritatis splendor,* no. 2.

has always taught, comes into being only through the free, irrevocable consent of a man and woman who, forswearing all others, freely give themselves to and are freely received by one another as husband and wife. If the man and the woman giving marital consent are Christians, this means that they are *already* members of Christ's Body, the Church; they are persons who have *already*, through baptism, become indissolubly one with Christ and his Spouse, the Church. As John Paul II noted earlier in the document, "by means of baptism, man and woman are definitively placed within the new and eternal covenant, in the spousal covenant of Christ with the Church" (no. 13). The point is that, through baptism, we become *new* persons, truly children of God and brothers and sisters of Jesus, called—and empowered—to love even as we have been and are loved by God in Christ (cf. Jn 13:34; 15:12–14; 1 Jn 3:16).[9] Through baptism, we "die" to sin and rise to a new kind of life in Christ; through baptism, we freely commit ourselves to live in union with Jesus and to share in his redemptive work. Our vocation as Christians is to complete, in our own flesh, "what is lacking in Christ's afflictions for the sake of his body, that is, the Church" (Col 1:24).[10]

Consequently, as John Paul II notes, "because of this indestructible insertion [of Christian men and women into the spousal covenant of Christ with the Church] . . . the intimate community of conjugal life and love, founded by the Creator, is elevated and assumed into the spousal charity of Christ, sustained and enriched by His redeeming power" (no. 13). It is for this reason that the deepest identity of the Christian family is that of a "Church in miniature (*Ecclesia domestica*)" (no. 49).[11] This identity is grounded in the reality of Christian marriage as a true sacrament.

[9] Here we must recall that the very principle of our lives as Christians is the *divine* love poured into our hearts when we are baptized. On this, see Germain Grisez, *The Way of the Lord Jesus*, vol. 1, *Christian Moral Principles* (Chicago: Franciscan Herald Press, 1983), chaps. 24 and 25.

[10] On the significance of baptism as the fundamental option of the Christian, the overarching free and self-determining choice of the Christian, see Grisez, *Christian Moral Principles*, chap. 23. See also John Paul II, Encyclical *Veritatis splendor*, no. 66.

[11] See also Vatican Council II, Dogmatic Constitution *Lumen gentium*, no. 11; Decree *Apostolicam actuositatem*, no. 11.

The Church's understanding of marriage as a sacrament in the precise sense of a created, visible reality that signifies and makes efficaciously present in the world the invisible reality of God's redemptive grace is rooted in its understanding of Christian marriage as a reality that not only *signifies*, as do all true marriages, the life-giving, love-giving, grace-giving union of Christ with his Bride, the Church, but also *inwardly participates* in this union. Those who believe in the Lord's Paschal Mystery and who have become, through his grace and the saving waters of baptism, living members of his Body know by faith that he has made their marriages the efficacious sign of his redemptive love for mankind. Just as the baptismal water both symbolizes life-giving power and actually gives divine life and the power to believe and hope and be children of God to those who receive it, and just as this water both symbolizes cleansing and actually takes away every sin brought to the font, so too does the marriage of Christians both symbolize and effectively make present the grace-giving love that Christ has for his Church in the lives of Christian spouses. It is precisely for this reason that the Christian family, rooted in the marriage of baptized men and women, is in truth a "Church in miniature".[12]

---

[12] On this, see Jean-Marie Aubert, "La Famille cellule d'Église", especially pp. 313–14: "On sait que l'idée même d'Église évoque celle de communauté structurée par amour-charité, communauté impliquant la participation de tous à la même vie divine. Or, si le mariage et la famille ont été à longuer de siècles, tout au long de la Révélation biblique, le symbole même du projet divin de sauver tous les hommes par une Alliance avec eux, ce symbole n'est pas devenu caduc avec la naissance de l'Église, bien au contraire. *La même typologie doit continuer à fonctionner:* la communauté famille est symbole de la communauté universelle de tous les hommes appelés à former le Peuple de Dieu autour du Christ, chef de cette humanité rachetée. Mais il y a plus. Du fait que desormais le mariage est élevé à la dignité de sacrement, source efficace de grace, ce symbolisme n'est pas uniquement représentatif, il est aussi de l'ordre de *l'accomplissement.* En d'autres termes, la famille doit être *un des lieux où se construit l'Église,* famille élargie de tous les croyants. Ce n'est donc pas seulement au plan de la croissance numérique du Royaume de Dieu que la famille tire sa dignité chrétienne, comme on la limite souvent. Mais c'est au plan lui-même de la vie de l'Église: du fait que le sacrement de mariage n'est pas un simple événement ponctuel, mais qu'il inaugure *un état de vie permanent,* la famille est un lieu privilégié de cette vie de grace, une véritable cellule de l'Église qui ... contribue à la vitalité et à l'expansion de toute l'Église."
On this, see also St. Thomas Aquinas, *Summa contra gentiles,* 4, 78.

Thus John Paul can rightly say that the marriage of Christian men and women "is the real representation, by means of the sacramental sign, of the very relationship of Christ with the Church" (no. 13). From this it follows, moreover, that

> [Christian] spouses are therefore the permanent reminder to the Church of what happened on the Cross; they are for one another and for their children witnesses to the salvation in which the sacrament makes them sharers. Of this salvation event marriage, like every sacrament, is a memorial, actuation, and prophecy: "As a memorial, the sacrament gives them the grace and duty of commemorating the great works of God and of bearing witness to them before their children. As actuation, it gives them the grace and duty of putting into practice in the present, towards each other and their children, the demands of a love which forgives and redeems. As prophecy, it gives them the grace and duty of living and bearing witness to the hope of the future encounter with Christ" (no. 13).[13]

All Christians, whether married or not, have, through baptism, freely committed themselves to share in Christ's redemptive work. But Christian spouses, whose marriage is sacramental precisely because it is the marriage of baptized persons, and the families founded on them have, John Paul II insists, a *specific and original role* to play in the drama of redemption. Christ himself has entrusted to the family, the "Church in miniature", the specific and indispensable role of building up "the kingdom of God in history *through the everyday realities that concern and distinguish its state of life. It is thus*", the Holy Father says, "in *the love between husband and wife and between the members of the family*—a love lived out in all its extraordinary richness of values and demands: totality, oneness, fidelity and fruitfulness—that the Christian family's participation in the prophetic, priestly and kingly mission of Jesus Christ and of his Church finds expression and realization" (no. 50). In short, it is by *realizing itself as such,* and not by any task superimposed on it,

[13] The internal citation is from John Paul II, "Address to the Delegates of the Centre de Liaison des Équipes de Recherche", November 3, 1979, p. 3; in *Insegnamenti di Giovanni Paolo II,* 2, no. 2 (1979): 1038.

that the Christian family acquits its specific and original ecclesial mission. Christian conjugal love, therefore, is the dynamic source of the Christian family's saving mission in the Church and for the Church.

2. Christian Conjugal Love as the Dynamic Source of the Christian Family's Saving Mission in the Church and for the Church

John Paul II insists that the Christian family builds up the Kingdom of God in history "through the everyday realities that concern and distinguish its *state of life*" (no. 50). He then concludes that "it is thus in *the love between husband and wife and between the members of the family*—a love lived out in all its extraordinary richness of values and demands: totality, oneness, fidelity and fruitfulness—that the Christian family's participation in the prophetic, priestly, and kingly mission of Jesus Christ and of his Church finds expression and realization. Therefore," he continues, "love and life constitute the nucleus of the saving mission of the Christian family in the Church and for the Church" (no. 50).

It is obvious that the love to which John Paul II here refers is the love specific to spouses—and to Christian spouses—for within this passage he explicitly refers to the teaching of Paul VI on the nature of conjugal love in his Encyclical *Humanae vitae* (no. 9), a text in which Paul himself summarized accurately the teaching set forth by Vatican Council II on the nature of this love (cf. *Gaudium et spes,* nos. 49–50). This love is characterized as one that is human, total, faithful and exclusive, and fruitful, and as a love proper and unique to spouses.

Earlier, in *Familiaris consortio,* John Paul II had emphasized that love is the *inner principle* of the family's life and mission. Indeed, he stressed that "*without love the family cannot live, grow and perfect itself as a community of persons"* (no. 18). He then said: "the love between husband and wife and, in a *derivatory* and broader way, the love between members of the same family—between parents and children, brothers and sisters and relatives and members of the household—is given life and sustenance by an unceasing inner dynamism leading the family to an ever deeper and more intense *communion,* which is the foundation and soul of the *community* of marriage and the family" (no. 18, emphasis in the original). Note that here John Paul II explicitly says that the love between parents and children, brothers and sisters and relatives and household members *derives* from the love specific to husband and wife, that is, from *conjugal love.* This is the love that is the life-giving principle of marriage and the inner dynamic principle giving to marriage and the family the capacity to carry out rightly its specific and original ecclesial role.

It is thus crucially important to have a proper understanding of the nature of conjugal love and its place within the structure of marriage. This understanding was beautifully expressed by the teaching of Vatican Council II in *Gaudium et spes,* a teaching wholeheartedly embraced and developed by John Paul II. Many, however, have gravely misinterpreted the teaching of Vatican Council II, claiming that the Council Fathers repudiated the traditional understanding that the procreation and education of children is the primary end of marriage and that it raised conjugal love to the level of an objective *end* of marriage, equal to if not superior to the procreation and education of children.[14] This interpretation of *Gaudium et spes* is, unfortunately, quite wide-spread today.

A careful study of the conciliar text, however, shows that this is

[14] See, for example, the following: V. Heylin, "La promozione della dignità del matrimonio e della famiglia", in *La Chiesa nel mondo di oggi (Studi e commenti intorno alla Costituzione pastorale) "Gaudium et spes"* (Florence: Vallacchi, 1966), p. 358; Theodore Mackin, *What Is Marriage?* (New York: Paulist Press, 1982), pp. 235–37, where he claims that Vatican Council II repudiated the teaching of Pius XII and instead adopted the view of Herbert Doms which had been censured by that pontiff; Michael Lawler, *Secular Marriage, Christian Sacrament* (Mystic, CT: Twenty-Third Publications, 1985), p. 53.

a gravely flawed interpretation.[15] It is true that the Council did not use the terminology of "primary" and "secondary" ends. But, as the *Acta* of the Council make clear, this was only because this technical and juridical terminology was judged inappropriate for a document of a pastoral nature. The *Acta* likewise make it clear that the definitive text submitted to the Council Fathers and accepted by them clearly identifies the procreation and the education of children as the primordial end of both the institution of marriage *and* conjugal love.[16]

Conjugal love is *never* described by the Council as an *end* of marriage. Rather, the *end* toward which conjugal love, as indeed the entire institution of marriage, is ordered is indeed the procreation and education of children (cf. *Gaudium et spes,* nos. 48, 50). The text of *Gaudium et spes* never speaks of conjugal love as an end of marriage; it does not even conceive it as a property of marriage. On the contrary, it consistently predicates of conjugal love the same ends (primordially, the procreation and education of children; subsidiarily, mutual help and assistance) and the same properties that it predicates of the whole institution of marriage.

[15] In my opinion, the best analysis of the teaching of *Gaudium et spes* on the proper place of conjugal love within the structure of marriage is Francisco Gil Hellin's "El lugar propio del amor conyugal en la estructura del matrimonio segun la 'Gaudium et spes' ", *Annales Valentinos* 6 (1980): 1–35. See also Gil Hellin, "El matrimonio: Amor e institucion", in *Cuestiones fundamentales sobre matrimonio y familia* (Il Simposio Internacional de Teologia de la Universidad de Navarra), Augusto Sarmiento et al., eds. (Pamplona: Eunsa, 1980); Ramón García de Haro, *Marriage and Family in the Documents of the Magisterium* trans. from the Italian by William E. May (San Francisco: Ignatius Press), pp. 234–56.

[16] See *Acta Synodalia,* vol. 4, pars 7, p. 472: Under c), the Council Commission says that "in a *pastoral* text which seeks to establish dialogue with the world these juridical elements ["primary" and "secondary" ends] are not required." Under f), the Commission notes that "many documents of tradition and the Magisterium are nonetheless cited [in the text] in which the discourse [*sermo*] concerns these goods and ends. [see fn. 1 of *Gaudium et spes,* no. 48 where reference is made to] St. Augustine, *De bono coniugii,* PL 40, 375–76 and 394; St. Thomas Aquinas, *Summa theologiae,* supplement, q. 49, art. 3, ad 1; *Decretum pro Armenis:* DS 1327; Pius XI, Encyclical *Casti connubii:* AAS 22 (1930): 547–48. . . . Moreover, the *primordial importance* [*momentum primordiale*] of the procreation and education of children is set forth at least ten times within the text. . . . "

Indeed, according to the thought of Vatican II, conjugal love is the *life-giving* principle of marriage, which the institution of marriage is designed to protect, precisely the same thought set forth by John Paul II in *Familiaris consortio*, no. 11. Conjugal love is indeed what constitutes the personal reality which the institution of marriage confirms, protects, and sanctions before God and man. This is central to the teaching of Vatican Council II, which affirmed that "from the conjugal covenant . . . that is, from the human act by which the spouses mutually give and receive each other, there arises in society an institution [marriage], confirmed by divine ordination; this holy bond (*hoc vinculum sacrum*), for the good of the spouses themselves, for the good of their children, and for the good of society, does not depend on human choice. God himself is the author of marriage, endowed with various goods and ends" (*Gaudium et spes,* no. 48). What this means is that the institution of marriage comes to be from an act of conjugal love — the act whereby the man and the woman irrevocably give themselves to each other as husband and wife — and the institution protects love, for true conjugal love is not limited or impeded by it, but rather both these elements, the institution of marriage and conjugal love, require and complete each other, as integrative elements of the one same reality: marriage or the conjugal community. As Francisco Gil Hellin has said, conjugal love and the institution of marriage "come to be in a mutual and essential dependence, and they constantly require each other: *love* has need of the institution in order to be conjugal, and the institution of marriage always implies a radical exigency to be enlivened by love."[17] John Paul II confirms this when he says:

> The only "place" in which this self-giving [the self-giving proper to conjugal love] in its whole truth is made possible is marriage, the covenant of conjugal love freely and consciously chosen, whereby man and woman accept the intimate community of life and love willed by God himself [cf. *Gaudium et spes,* no. 48]. . . . The institution of marriage is not an undue interference by society or authority. . . . Rather it is an interior require-

<hr/>

[17] Gil Hellin, "El lugar propio del amor conyugal", p. 35.

ment of the covenant of conjugal love (*Familiaris consortio,* no. 11).

But what is conjugal love? According to the teaching of Vatican Council II, conjugal love is not a passion or mere sentiment but that "eminently human" affection which proceeds from free will and assumes into itself, ennobling them, all the natural tendencies of the person: "That love, as eminently human, since it is directed from one person to another person by an affection rooted in the will, embraces the good of the whole person and therefore is capable of enriching with a peculiar dignity the manifestations of both mind and body and of ennobling them as elements and special signs of conjugal friendship" (*Gaudium et spes,* no. 49). Continuing, in a most important passage, the Council Fathers go on to say: "Our Lord has deigned to heal, perfect, and elevate this love with a special gift of grace and of charity. A love like this, bringing together the human and the divine, leads the spouses to the free and mutual gift of themselves, experienced in tender affection and action, and permeates the whole of their lives [cf. Pius XI, Encyclical *Casti connubii:* AAS 22 (1930): 547–48]; moreover, this love is perfected and grows by its generous exercise" (no. 49). God's grace, therefore, perfects the nature of conjugal love, establishing marriage as a sacrament and married life as a divine vocation (no. 49).

Conjugal love is characterized by the properties of unity and indissolubility. Already on the plane of nature—of God the Creator's plan—it has this requirement: "This intimate union, as the mutual giving of two persons, as well as the good of the children, demand the full fidelity of the spouses and require their indissoluble unity" (*Gaudium et spes,* no. 48). And both these properties of conjugal love are confirmed and ratified by grace: "Christ remains with them [the spouses], so that just as he loved the Church and gave himself up for her, so too the spouses, by their mutual self-giving, may love each other with perpetual fidelity" (no. 48). Indeed, "this love, endorsed by mutual fidelity, and above all consecrated by Christ's sacrament, is indissolubly faithful amidst prosperity and adversity of both the body and of the spirit, and consequently remains foreign to every kind of adultery and divorce. The unity of marriage, confirmed by the Lord, shines forth brilliantly in the equal personal dignity which must be given to man and wife in mutual and unreserved love" (*Gaudium et spes,* no. 49).

And finally, *Gaudium et spes* teaches that *conjugal love has as its intrinsic end the procreation and education of children* (cf. *Gaudium et spes,* nos. 48, 50). Indeed, the Council insists that "the true cultivation of conjugal love and the whole structure of family life arising therefrom, without neglecting the other ends of marriage, tend to this, that the spouses are disposed by a courageous spirit to cooperate with the love of the Creator and Redeemer, who through them will day by day increase and enrich his family" (*Gaudium et spes,* no. 50). Indeed, one of the most novel affirmations of *Gaudium et spes,* one which marks true theological development on the matter, is that conjugal love, and not only marriage as an institution, has as its end the procreation and education of children.

> What distinguishes the text, in relationship to the previous Magisterium on the ends of marriage, is that it distinguishes between two formally diverse elements contained in the conjugal community [the institution of marriage and conjugal love]. It thus makes explicit 'the significance of conjugal love even for the procreating and educating of children.'[18]

While up to now the Magisterium of the Church affirmed that marriage "tends toward the procreation and education of children", Vatican Council II tells us that both the institutional aspect and conjugal love "tend toward the procreation and education of children".[19]

Conjugal love, therefore, is regarded by Vatican Council II and by John Paul II as the inner principle of marriage and of the vocation of married couples. Conjugal love is thus essential to

---

[18] García de Haro, p. 244. Here see *Acta Synodalia,* vol. 4, pars 1, p. 536, *Relatio ad Schema receptum:* "Mentio fit duo, uti multi patres petierunt, de matrimonio simul et amore. Momentum etiam amoris coniugalis etiam ad ipsam procreandam educandamque sublineatur."

[19] Gil Hellin, "El lugar propio del amor conyugal", p. 16.

marriage. This does not, however, mean that, should conjugal love "die", the marriage dies.[20] As we have seen, the first act of conjugal love is the act of irrevocable personal consent whereby the man and the woman unconditionally and irrevocably give themselves to each other as husband and wife. Conjugal love is included in the object of their consent, as the Christian tradition has consistently taught.[21] In the conjugal community, conjugal love is the life-giving principle owed by virtue of the very consent that has generated it. Nonetheless, its absence from a marriage does not destroy it. This is so because marriage, while born from the human act that brings it into being, does not depend upon their arbitrary will (cf. *Gaudium et spes,* no. 48). Therefore, the unjust and unlawful violation later on of the requirements of love cannot annul either the consent or the community, as Vatican Council II insisted.[22] Within the conjugal community conjugal love is an essential good, existing at least as a *requirement.* Moreover, for Christian spouses, there is the assurance that God and Christ, who led them *to* marriage, are with them *in* marriage, ever ready to enable them to give one another the conjugal love that is the life-giving principle of marriage and of the mission that has been entrusted to them. This love finds its fulfillment in the mutual sanctification of the spouses, a sanctification that requires them to carry out rightly the threefold mission that has been entrusted to them, the mission to which I shall now turn.

---

[20] This, unfortunately, is the claim of some contemporary theologians. See, for instance, Mackin, p. 315, where he writes: "Since, according to *Gaudium et spes,* a marriage is to be understood as an intimate community of life and marital love, it can dissolve and disintegrate."

[21] See, for instance, St. Augustine, *De bono coniugali,* cap. 3, no. 3; PL 40, 375; St. Thomas Aquinas, *Summa theologiae,* supplement, q. 49, a. 3.

[22] See *Gaudium et spes,* no. 48. *Acta Synodalia,* vol. 4, pars 1, p. 536: *Relatio ad Schema receptum:* "Notio instituti matrimonii sequenti phrasi firmatur, ne ullus censeat sese illud arbitrio suo postea dissolver posse; aut, deficiente amore etiam requisito, matrimonium suum nullum fieri."

3. The Substantive Content of the Christian Family's Role: Participating in the Prophetic, Priestly, Kingly Missions of Christ.

As far as the substantive content of this mission is concerned, John Paul II uses the scheme of participation in the threefold mission of Christ as Prophet, Priest, and King and thus presents the Christian family under the threefold aspect of being a believing and evangelizing community, a community in dialogue with God, and a community at the service of mankind.

The family as a believing and evangelizing community: its prophetic role. The Christian family shares in Christ's prophetic mission "by welcoming and announcing the word of God" (no. 51). Thus the first requirement of Christian spouses and parents is faith, because "only in faith can they discover and admire with joyful gratitude the dignity to which God has deigned to raise marriage and the family, making them a sign and meeting place of the loving covenant between God and man, between Jesus Christ and his bride, the Church" (no. 51). The driving force of the Christian family is, as we have seen, the love specific to spouses, but Christian spouses know through faith that their love is a sign and real participation in the love of God and in his redemptive power. God, who through faith "called the couple *to* marriage, continues to call them *in* marriage" (no. 51).[23] "In and through the events, problems, difficulties, and circumstances of everyday life, God comes to them, revealing and presenting the concrete 'demands' of their sharing in the love of Christ for his Church in the particular family, social, and ecclesial situation in which they find themselves" (no. 51).

Faith thus heard and experienced in love makes the Christian family a fire that sheds its light on many other families (cf. no. 52). This prophetic mission of the family, John Paul II emphasizes, is the dynamic expression of its inner identity; the family carries this

[23] Here John Paul II explicitly refers to what Paul VI had taught in *Humanae vitae*, no. 25.

mission out by being faithful to its own proper being as a community of life and love: the "apostolic mission of the family is rooted in baptism and receives from the grace of the sacrament of marriage new strength to transmit the faith, to sanctify and transform our present society according to God's plan" (no. 52).

The Pope notes two characteristics of the prophetic apostolate of the family. First of all, it is exercised within the family itself by encouraging and helping family members to live fully their Christian vocation. Wisely, the Holy Father notes that "just as in the Church the work of evangelization can never be separated from the sufferings of the apostle, so in the Christian family parents must face with courage and great interior serenity the difficulties that their ministry of evangelization sometimes encounters in their own children" (no. 53). In addition, this prophetic and evangelizing apostolate, begun within the family itself, includes the "task of defending and spreading the faith, a task that has its roots in baptism and confirmation, and makes Christian married couples and parents witnesses of Christ 'to the ends of the earth', missionaries, in the true and proper sense, of love and life" (no. 54). One form of this missionary activity, John Paul II observes, "can be exercised even within the family. This happens when some member of the family does not have the faith or does not practice it with consistency. In such a case the other members must give him or her a living witness of their own faith in order to encourage and support him or her along the path towards full acceptance of Christ the Savior" (no. 54).

The family as a community in dialogue with God: its priestly role. John Paul II begins his presentation of this essential task of the Christian family by reminding us that marriage is a sacrament of mutual sanctification and of worship and that the love of Christian spouses has been judged by the Lord, as Vatican Council II had noted earlier, "worthy of special gifts, healing, perfecting and exalting gifts of grace and of charity" (no. 56).[24] Moreover, "the gift of Jesus Christ is not exhausted in the actual celebration of the

---

24 The internal citation is taken from Vatican Council II, *Gaudium et spes*, no. 49.

sacrament of marriage, but rather accompanies the married couple throughout their lives" (no. 56).

Precisely because Christian marriage is a sacrament of mutual sanctification, the universal call of all Christians to holiness is, for Christian spouses and parents, "specified by the sacrament they have celebrated and is carried out concretely in the realities proper to their conjugal and family life" (no. 56). John Paul II then emphasizes the *sacramental foundation* of the sanctity demanded of spouses. Holiness is not easy, and it lies beyond merely human powers. To sanctify themselves, their children, and the world in which they live, Christian spouses must have recourse to the sources of divine grace, in particular the Eucharist and confession. Just as love is the proper power of the family and participation in Christ's love is what defines the Christian family, so the Eucharist is the living fountain of Christian married and family life: "The Eucharist is the very source of Christian marriage. The Eucharistic Sacrifice, in fact, represents Christ's covenant of love with the Church, sealed by his blood on the cross. . . . The Eucharist is a fountain of charity. In the Eucharistic gift of charity the Christian family finds the foundation and soul of its 'communion' and 'mission' " (no. 57).[25] In addition, it is through the sacrament of penance that "the married couple and the other members of the family are led to an encounter with God, who is 'rich in mercy', who bestows on them his love which is more powerful than sin, and who reconstructs and brings to perfection the marriage covenant and the family communion" (no. 58).

By keeping close to Christ through the sacraments of the Eucharist and of penance and by prayer, the Christian family can discover family life itself, in all its circumstances,

> as a call from God and as a filial response to his call. Joys and sorrows, hopes and disappointments, births and birthday celebrations, wedding anniversaries of the parents, departures, separations and homecomings, important and far-reaching decisions, the death of those who are dear, etc.—all of these mark God's

[25] On this see Michele Marie Herbst, "The Eucharistic Meaning of Marriage", *Anthropotes* 10 (1994), pp. 164–76.

loving intervention in the family's history. They should be seen as suitable moments for thanksgiving, for petition, for trusting abandonment of the family into the hands of their common Father in heaven (no. 59).

The family as a community at the service of mankind: its kingly role. The Christian family exercises this role by putting itself at the service of others, as Christ did and as he asks his disciples to do (no. 63). Here the Holy Father stresses that "the law of Christian life is to be found not in a written code but in the personal action of the Holy Spirit who inspires and guides the Christian" (no. 63). For Christian spouses and their families, the guide and rule of life is the Spirit of Jesus, the evangelical law of love (no. 63). Thus, "inspired and sustained by the new commandment of love, the Christian family welcomes, respects, and serves every human being, considering each one in his or her dignity as a person and a child of God" (no. 64). This profound respect for the dignity of human persons must be shown first of all within the family itself—between husband and wife and their children,

> through a daily effort to promote a truly personal community, initiated and fostered by an inner communion of love. This way of life should then be extended to the wider circle of the ecclesial community of which the Christian family is a part . . . [and ultimately this] love goes beyond our brothers and sisters of the same faith since "everybody is my brother or sister." In each individual, especially in the poor, the weak, and those who suffer or are unjustly treated, love knows how to discover the face of Christ and to discover a fellow human being to be loved and served (no. 64).

APPENDIX
Pope John Paul II's *Letter to Families:*
An Overview

Pope John Paul II's *Letter to Families,* dated February 2, 1994, was written to express the Church's concern for families during the International Year of the Family. The *Letter* contains an Introduction (numbered sections 1–5) and two major parts: 1: The Civilization of Love (numbered sections 6–17), and 2: The Bridegroom Is with You (numbered sections 18–23). In it, the Holy Father, who has throughout his entire life as a priest and in a special way throughout his pontificate devoted extraordinary attention to marriage and family, speaks passionately about the absolutely indispensable role that the family, rooted in the marriage of one man and one woman, has to play in the "civilization of love". His burning desire is to awaken in the hearts and minds of men and women, and in particular in the hearts and minds of Christian spouses, an understanding of and commitment to the sublime mission entrusted by God to families, to encourage husbands and wives to be faithful to their vocation, and to defend the family from the dangers threatening it today.

Here I will try to provide an overview of Pope John Paul II's *Letter* by focusing on the following themes developed in it: (1) the meaning of the "civilization of love"; (2) marriage as the "rock" upon which the family is built precisely because it is a person-affirming, love-enabling, life-giving, and sanctifying reality; and (3) the family and society.

The Meaning of the "Civilization of Love"

"The civilization of love", the Holy Father writes, "originates in the revelation of the God who 'is love' (cf. 1 Jn 4:8, 16) . . . and it grows as a result of the *constant cultivation* which the Gospel allegory of the vine and the branches describes in such a direct way: 'I am the true vine, and my Father is the vinedresser. Every branch of mine that bears no fruit, he takes away, and every branch that bears fruit he prunes, so that it may bear more fruit' (Jn 15:1–2)" (no. 13).

God, who "is love", created man out of love and for love. "[A]lone of all creatures, man, male and female, was created in the image and likeness of God (Gen 1:26–27)" (no. 6), from whose hands "he has received the world . . . together with the task of shaping it in his own image and likeness. The fulfillment of this task gives rise to civilization, which in the final analysis is nothing else than the 'humanization of the world' " (no. 13).

Moreover, and most importantly, the Holy Father, citing from Vatican Council II's Pastoral Constitution on the Church in the Modern World, *Gaudium et spes,* reminds us, " 'by his incarnation the Son of God united himself in a certain way to every man' (*Gaudium et spes,* no. 22) . . . [and in fact] 'fully discloses man to himself' (*Gaudium et spes,* no. 22)" (no. 2). From this it follows that the civilization of love culminates in the redemptive, self-giving love of God which has been fully revealed to us in the life, death, and Resurrection of his only begotten Son. As a being made by the God who is love and as a being whose vocation is to love even as we have been and are loved by God in Christ, man, male and female, can find himself, fulfill himself, only through love, which essentially consists in the "sincere gift of self" (no. 11; cf. *Gaudium et spes,* no. 24).

And *"the family is fundamental to . . . the 'civilization of love' "* (no. 13). The family, in fact, *"is the center and heart of the civilization of love",* a civilization completely dependent on the truth about man and his vocation (no. 13). But what is the family, and why is it the center and heart of the civilization of love?

Marriage: The "Rock" on Which the Family Is Built

The Holy Father says that his *Letter* is "in the first place . . . a prayer to Christ to remain in every human family", that "prayer should be first of all an encouraging witness on the part of those families who live out their human and Christian vocation in the communion of the home" and that "with reason it can be said that these families make up *'the norm'*, even admitting the existence of more than a few 'irregular situations'." Continuing, he says that "experience shows what an important role is played by a family living in accordance with the moral norm, so that the individual born and raised in it will be able to set out without hesitation on the road of the good, which is *always written in the heart*" (no. 5).

The family "living in accordance with the moral norm" is the family built upon the marriage of one man and one woman. Indeed, "marriage, which undergirds the institution of the family, is constituted by the covenant whereby 'a man and a woman establish between themselves a partnership of their whole life', and which 'of its own very nature is ordered to the well-being of the spouses and to the procreation and upbringing of children' (*Code of Canon Law*, can. 1055, par. 1; *Catechism of the Catholic Church*, no. 1601). Only such a union", John Paul II affirms, "can be recognized and ratified as a 'marriage' in society. Other interpersonal unions which do not fulfill the above conditions cannot be recognized, despite certain growing trends which represent a serious threat to the future of the family and of society itself" (no. 17).

This is the family whose *"primordial model"*, as we can see "[i]n the light of the New Testament", "*is to be sought in God himself*, in the Trinitarian mystery of his life. The divine 'We' is the eternal pattern of the human 'we', especially of that 'we' formed by the man and the woman created in the divine image and likeness" (no. 6). For marriage is God's great gift to mankind, created by him and given its defining characteristics by him in the act of creating man, male and female. This is precisely the meaning of the first chapters of Genesis, which John Paul II elsewhere speaks of as the narratives relating the "beatifying beginning" of the human race.[1] The marriage of one man and one woman is the "rock" on which the family in its normative sense is built, because marriage is a *person-affirming, love-enabling,* and *life-giving reality.* Moreover, because this beautiful human reality has been raised by Christ to the dignity of a sacrament of the new law of love, it is also a *sanctifying reality.*

As discussed in Chapter One, marriage is a person-affirming reality because it is "covenant of persons in love" (no. 7). It comes into existence when a man and a woman, forswearing all others, *give themselves to each other irrevocably as husband and wife.* It is rooted in a free, self-determining choice whereby the man, in giving himself unconditionally to this particular woman and in being freely received by her, gives to himself the identity of her *husband* and to her the identity of his *wife,* whereby the woman, in freely receiving this particular man and in giving herself unconditionally to him, gives to herself the identity of his *wife* and to him the identity of her *husband,* and whereby both the man and woman give to themselves irrevocably the identity of *spouses.*

As John Paul II notes in his *Letter,* free choice is at the heart of marital consent, a choice made possible only because man—male and female—has the identity of a person capable of *"living in truth and in love"* (no. 8). That free choice is at the heart of marital consent is clearly brought out, he observes, in the second chapter of Genesis (no. 8).

In Chapter One I emphasized that the indissolubility of marriage is ontologically grounded, i.e., grounded in the very *being* of husband and wife. It is so grounded because it is rooted in the *identity* that they have freely chosen to give to themselves in choosing to marry, i.e., to give themselves irrevocably to one another in marriage and to make themselves *to be* husbands and wives, spouses.

---

[1] Pope John Paul II, "Nuptial Meaning of the Body", General Audience of January 9, 1980, in *Original Unity of Man and Woman: Catechesis on Genesis* (Boston: St. Paul Editions, 1981), p. 103. In this address, the Holy Father is explicitly speaking about the Yahwist narrative of creation in Genesis 2, but his words also apply to the Priestly narrative in Genesis 1.

John Paul II brings this out in his *Letter* when he emphasizes that husband and wife have, in marrying, made the "sincere gift of self" to one another, and that "the indissolubility of marriage flows . . . from the very essence of that gift" (no. 11). Because they have *irrevocably* made the "sincere gift of self" to one another, they simply cannot take that gift away. The indissoluble character of marriage, the Holy Father reminds us, "[is] the *basis of the common good of the family*" (no. 7).

Marriage, a love-enabling reality, comes into existence *through* an act of love, through the "*sincere gift of one person to another person*. . . . Without this [sincere gift of one person to another person] marriage would be empty, whereas a communion of persons [is] built upon this logic" (no. 11). In marriage "man and woman are so firmly united as to become . . . 'one flesh' (Gen 2:24). Male and female in their physical constitution, the two human subjects, even though physically different, *share equally in the capacity to live 'in truth and in love'* . . . and thus express the maturity proper to persons created in the image and likeness of God" (no. 8).

And marriage enables husband and wife to give one another the love unique and exclusive to spouses, namely, conjugal love, which is human, total, faithful and exclusive until death, and fertile.[2] Indeed, the deepening of conjugal love is an integral aspect of the common good of marriage and the family. "The words of [marital] consent", John Paul II affirms, "define the common good of the *couple and of the family*. First, the common good of the spouses: love, fidelity, honor, the permanence of their union until death—'all the days of my life' " (no. 10).

The depths of conjugal love, made possible by marriage, are revealed by Jesus himself. Jesus identified himself as the "Bridegroom" (cf. Mt 9:15). By doing so, the Holy Father points out, "Jesus reveals the essence of God and confirms his immense love for mankind. But the choice of this image also throws light indirectly on the profound truth of spousal love. Indeed, by using

---

[2] On this, see Vatican Council II, *Gaudium et spes*, nos. 49–50, and Pope Paul VI, Encyclical *Humanae vitae*, no. 9.

this image in order to speak about God, Jesus shows to what extent the fatherhood and the love of God are reflected in the love of a man and a woman united in marriage" (no. 18). He began his public ministry at Cana in Galilee, taking part in a wedding banquet. By doing so, "he thus wishes to make clear *to what extent the truth about the family is part of God's Revelation and the history of salvation*.... At Cana in Galilee Jesus is, as it were, the *herald of the divine truth about marriage*, the truth on which the human family can rely, gaining reassurance amid all the trials of life" (no. 18). Moreover, he "proclaims the truth about marriage again when, speaking to the Pharisees, he explains how the love which comes from God, a tender and spousal love, *gives rise to profound and radical demands*" (no. 18).

Spousal love, beautiful and tender, is a *demanding* love, requiring husbands and wives to be utterly faithful to one another and to grow ever more deeply in their exclusive love for one another, which is an integral part of the common good of marriage and the family. Spousal love is, in fact, the *life-giving principle* or form of marriage. Within the conjugal community—the *communio personarum* (cf. no. 7)—established by the act of marital consent, spousal love abides as its life-giving principle, owed by virtue of the very consent that has generated it. As Vatican Council II put the matter: "the intimate union [of the spouses], as the mutual gift of persons, as well as the good of the children . . . *require* the full fidelity of the spouses and *demand* their indissoluble unity."[3] This love, "ratified by mutual faith", must be "indissolubly faithful amidst the prosperities and adversities of both body and spirit".[4]

Additionally, and this is of paramount significance, husbands and wives, who are *required* to give to one another spousal love, are capable of doing so *because they are married*. Marriage, in other words, *enables* them to give this kind of love to one another.[5]

---

[3] Vatican Council II, *Gaudium et spes*, no. 48, par. 1.

[4] Ibid., no. 49, par. 2.

[5] On spousal love as the life-giving principle of marriage and on marriage as a

Husbands and wives can fulfill themselves, become fully the beings God wills them to be, only if they shape their married lives in accordance with the truth: and the truth is that they have become "one flesh" through their own free and self-determining choice. Their marital union is an earthly image of the *communio personarum* that is the triune God. With the never-failing help of Christ, who is, as St. Thomas reminds us, "our best and wisest friend",[6] they can be true to their marital commitment. *"The Bridegroom is with them"*, as our Holy Father emphasizes in his loving *Letter to Families* (no. 18).

Precisely because marriage is a *love-enabling* reality "[t]he 'civilization of love' ... bound up with the family" is not, the Holy Father emphasizes, a "utopia". It is not a utopia because love "is entrusted to man and woman, in the Sacrament of Matrimony, as the basic principle of their 'duty', and it becomes the foundation of their mutual responsibility: first as spouses, then as father and mother. ... *Through the family passes the primary current of the civilization of love,* which finds therein its 'social foundations'" (no. 15).

Marriage is also a life-giving reality. The triune God is the Lord and Giver of life. And the human family, rooted in the marriage of one man and one woman, "has its origin", John Paul II declares, "in the same love with which the Creator embraces the created world. ... [In fact], [t]he *only-begotten Son*, of one substance with the Father, 'God from God, and Light from Light', *entered into human history through the family*" (no. 2).

Marriage "has to do with the personal relationship between the 'I' and the 'thou' ", with their intimate union of conjugal love (no.

reality that enables a man and a woman to give each other this kind of love, see Ramón García de Haro, *Marriage and Family in the Documents of the Magisterium*, trans. William E. May (San Francisco: Ignatius Press, 1993), pp. 234–56. See also Francisco Gil Hellin, "El lugar propio del amor conyugal en la estructura del matrimonio segun la 'Gaudium et spes' ", in *Annales Valentinos* 6, no. 11 (1980): 1–35.

[6] St. Thomas Aquinas, *Summa theologiae*, 1–2, 108, 4, sed contra: "Christus est maxime sapiens et amicus."

7). Community, as distinct from communion, "transcends this framework and moves towards a 'society', a 'we'. The family, as a community of persons, is thus the first human 'society'. It arises whenever there comes into being the conjugal covenant of marriage, which opens the spouses to a lasting communion of love and of life, and it is brought to completion in a full and specific way with the procreation of children: the 'communion' of the spouses gives rise to the 'community' of the family" (no. 7).

The procreation and education of children is an integral component of the common good to which spouses are committed. Conjugal love is a fertile, life-giving love. When husband and wife "transmit *life to a child, a new human 'thou' becomes a part of the horizon of the 'we' of the spouses...*" (no. 11). In fact, the Pope rightly observes, "*in the newborn child* is realized the common good of the family.... The child becomes a gift to its brothers, sisters, parents, and entire family. *Its life becomes a gift for the very people who were givers of life* and who cannot help feel its presence, its sharing in their life and its contribution to their common good and to that of the community and the family" (no. 11). Children are indeed, as the Fathers of Vatican Council II said, "the supreme gift of marriage".[7]

The Holy Father, in a section of his *Letter* concerned with "the genealogy of the person", beautifully describes the sublime mission of giving life to new human persons that God has entrusted to married men and women, husbands and wives, who are called to be fathers and mothers. He writes as follows:

Bound up with the family is the genealogy of every individual: *the genealogy of the person.* Human fatherhood and motherhood are rooted in biology, yet at the same time transcend it.... Every act of begetting finds its primordial model in the fatherhood of God.... When a new person is born of the conjugal union of the two, he brings with him into the world a particular image and likeness of God himself: *the genealogy of the person is inscribed in the very biology of generation....* God himself is present in human fatherhood and motherhood quite differently than he is present in

---

[7] Vatican Council II, *Gaudium et spes,* no. 50.

all other instances of begetting "on earth" as the sole source of a new image and likeness of himself. Begetting is the continuation of Creation. And so, both in the conception and birth of a new child, parents find themselves face to face with a "great mystery" (cf. Eph 5:32). Like his parents, the *new human being is also called* to live as a person; he is called *to a life "in truth and in love"*.... From the very moment of conception, and then of birth, the new human being is meant *to express fully his humanity,* to "find himself" as a person. [And God wills] *to lavish upon man a sharing in his own divine life....* By his very genealogy, the person created in the image and likeness of God *exists "for his own sake",* and reaches fulfillment precisely by *sharing in God's life....* [Parents must therefore] *want the new human creature in the same way as the Creator wants him:* "for himself" (no. 9).

Marriage, precisely because it is a communion of persons united by spousal love, is by its very nature ordered to the procreation and education of children. It enables husbands and wives not only to welcome new life lovingly but also to give it a home where it can take root and grow in the "civilization of love".

Spousal love is intrinsically life-giving, and the intimate union of husband and wife in the marital act is indissolubly both unitive and procreative. "Husband and wife are called to confirm in a responsible way *the mutual gift* of self which they made to each other in the marriage covenant. The logic of the *total gift of self to the other*", John Paul II affirms, "involves a potential openness to procreation.... *The intimate truth of this gift* must always be *safeguarded*" (no. 12).

If a couple were deliberately to do something to impede the communication of spousal love, they would be acting in a non-marital way; they would not be open to the gift of marital love. Likewise, if they were deliberately to do something, either prior to their marital embrace, during it, or subsequent to it, precisely to impede the handing on of human life,[8] their union would not truly be marital. It would be both an anti-love act inasmuch as they would not truly be "giving" themselves fully

---

[8] This is precisely the way Pope Paul VI defines contraception in *Humanae vitae,* no. 14. See above, Chapter Three.

and unreservedly to one another,[9] and it would be an anti-life act inasmuch as its precise point is to impede the beginning of a new human life; should new life be given despite the effort to impede it, it would come into the world as "unwanted". It would not be "lovingly received" as it ought to be.[10]

In educating the new life that God has given to them, parents are God's very own coworkers. Indeed, "[t]hrough Christ all education . . . *becomes part of God's own saving pedagogy*, which . . . culminates in the Paschal Mystery of the Lord's death and resurrection" (no. 16). Children are to "honor" their parents. "Honor is essentially", John Paul II says, "an attitude to unselfishness . . . a 'sincere gift of person to person'." And not only should children honor the parents who have, through God's will, given them life, their mothers and fathers "should act in such a way that [their] life *will merit the honor* of [their] children" (no. 15).

Marriage, which has its source in God, the Lord and Giver of life, is indeed a *life-giving* reality.

John Paul II's *Letter* shows marriage also to be a sanctifying reality. The Holy Father, as already noted, emphasizes that Jesus, by identifying himself as a "Bridegroom", not only "reveals the essence of God and confirms his immense love for mankind" but also "throws light . . . on the profound truth of spousal love". The author of the Epistle to the Ephesians considers marriage a great mystery "because it expresses *the spousal love of Christ for his Church* (cf. Eph 5:32)" (no. 19). Husbands are to love their wives as Christ loved the Church "and gave himself up for her, that he might

[9] Pope John Paul II has frequently developed this idea during his pontificate, namely, that contraception by a married couple violates conjugal love and makes the marital act a "lie" insofar as it simulates and does not truly express the sincere gift of self. An excellent summary of his thought on this subject is provided by Janet Smith, *Humanae Vitae: A Generation Later* (Washington, DC: The Catholic University of America Press, 1991), pp. 230–65.

[10] For a development of this theme, see Germain Grisez, Joseph Boyle, John Finnis, and William E. May, " 'Every Marital Act Ought to Be Open to New Life': Toward a Clearer Understanding", *Thomist* 52 (1988): 365–426. This essay is also found in the book by these authors and John Ford, S.J., *The Teaching of "Humanae Vitae": A Defense* (San Francisco: Ignatius Press, 1988).

sanctify her, having cleansed her by the washing of water and with the word" (Eph 5:25-26).

Commenting on this passage, John Paul II says that here the Apostle Paul is talking about baptism, "which he discusses at length in the Letter to the Romans, where he presents it as a sharing in the death of Christ leading to a sharing in his life (cf. Rom 6:3-4). In this Sacrament [baptism] the believer *is born* as a new man, for Baptism has the power to communicate new life, the very life of God" (no. 19). Christian husbands and wives thus find in Christ, the Pope says, *"the point of reference for their spousal love.... The 'great mystery', which is the Church and humanity in Christ, does not exist apart from the 'great mystery' expressed in the 'one flesh' (cf. Gen 2:24; Eph 5:31-32), that is, in the reality of marriage and the family"* (no. 19).

Thus it is that the family based on the sacramental marriage of Christians husbands and wives is in truth a "domestic Church" (no. 19). It has been commissioned by Christ himself, as John Paul II had earlier explained at length in his Apostolic Exhortation *Familiaris consortio,* to participate in a unique and indispensable way in the saving mission of the universal Church. It is to do this by sharing profoundly in Christ's threefold mission as Prophet, Priest, and King and by being a believing and evangelizing community, a community in dialogue with God, and a community serving others by transforming the world through the redemptive love of Christ.[11]

Because marriage is a *sanctifying* reality, the family built on it intimately shares in the "history of 'fairest love' ", a history that began, in a certain way, with the first human couple and culminated paradigmatically in the marital union of Mary and Joseph, thanks to whom "the *mystery of the Incarnation* and, together with it, the mystery of the Holy Family, *come to be profoundly inscribed in the spousal love of husband and wife*" (no. 20). Marriage is indeed a *sanctifying* reality.

---

[11] On this see Pope John Paul II, *Familiaris consortio,* nos. 49-64. For a commentary, see Chapter Five above.

The Family and Society

The family is the "basic cell" of society (no. 4). It is the "first and basic expression of man's *social nature*" (no. 7). The family, "more than any other human reality", is "the place where an individual can exist 'for himself' through the sincere gift of self. This is why it remains a social institution which neither can nor should be replaced: it is the 'sanctuary of life' " (no. 11; cf. Encyclical *Centessimus annus*, no. 39). It is *"the center and heart of the civilization of love"* (no. 13). Because it is all this, the family renders the larger human society an absolutely indispensable and priceless service.

The family built upon the marriage of one man and one woman thus expects from society *"a recognition of its identity* and an acceptance of its *status as a subject in society"* (no. 17). It has its own sovereignty, albeit conditioned, and it must be respected for what it is. It is the bearer of rights within society that must be honored. While the rights of the family are intimately linked to the inviolable rights of persons, they are, John Paul II insists, *"not simply the sum total* of the rights of the person, since the family is *much more* than the sum of individual members. It is a community of parents and children, and at times a community of several generations. For this reason", he continues, "its 'status as a subject', which is grounded in God's plan, gives rise to and calls for certain proper and specific rights" (no. 17).

Here I cannot go into detail with respect to the rights of the family that must be respected by the international community, the nation, and the State: rights such as those of the parents to procreate and to educate their own children, to a living wage, and so on. Yet it is important, in coming to a close of this overview of Pope John Paul II's *Letter to Families,* to focus on two issues. The first of these concerns the rights of women and mothers. The Holy Father is particularly eloquent about these rights. He stresses the importance of acknowledging and appreciating the *"work women do within the family unit".* He writes:

> The "toil" of a woman who, having given birth to a child, nourishes and cares for that child and devotes herself to its

upbringing, particularly in the early years, is so great as to be comparable to any professional work. This ought to be clearly stated and upheld, no less than any other labor right. Motherhood, because of all the hard work it entails, should be recognized as giving the right to financial benefits at least equal to those of other kinds of work undertaken in order to support the family during such a delicate phase of its life (no. 17).

The second concerns the terrible dangers facing families built upon marriage today. John Paul II is emphatic and correct in declaring that the marriage of one man and one woman is the rock on which the family is built and that only a union of this kind can be recognized and ratified as marriage in society. But today there is, on the part of some powerful elites, an attempt to confer the dignity of marriage—along with the rights pertaining to it—to unions of "free love", that is, unions that endure only so long as they are pleasing to their partners, and even to homosexual liaisons. Referring to this growing tendency, John Paul II vigorously declares that "[n]o human society can run the risk of permissiveness in fundamental issues regarding the nature of marriage and the family! Such moral permissiveness cannot fail to damage the authentic requirements of peace and communion among people" (no. 17).

In his *Letter,* the Holy Father identifies some of the basic dangers to family life today: a rampant individualism utterly opposed to true personalism (cf. no. 14), the ethic of utilitarianism that treats persons as an object of use (cf. no. 14), a dualism reminiscent of the ancient ideologies of gnosticism and Manichaeanism (cf. no. 19). All these evils encourage selfishness and hedonism, give rise to the plague of divorce and the anti-life mentality so manifest in the widespread practice of contraception and abortion. In many ways, human society today, the Holy Father points out, is "sick", because it has lost sight of the truth about man, the truth "about what man and woman really are as persons" (no. 20). The "civilization of love" is threatened by a "civilization of death". But we are to have hope, because the *Bridegroom is with us.* If we abide in God's love, honor marriage and the family built on it, we can develop the "civilization of love", a civilization in which all human persons, born or unborn, of whatever condition or race or sex, will indeed be wanted and loved as a person made in the image and likeness of God and called to life eternal as a member of God's own family.

INDEX